Cross-Departmental Challenges

A Whole-of-Government Approach
for the Twenty-First Century

Patrick Whelan
Tom Arnold
Agnes Aylward
Mary Doyle
Bernadette Lacey
Claire Loftus
Nuala McLoughlin
Eamonn Molloy
Jennifer Payne
Melanie Pine

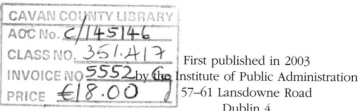
First published in 2003
by the Institute of Public Administration
57–61 Lansdowne Road
Dublin 4
Ireland

© The authors

ISBN 1 904541 03 8

British Library cataloguing-in-publication data
A catalogue record for this book is available
from the British Library

Cover design by Butler Claffey Design, Dún Laoghaire
Typeset in Garamond 11/12.5 by Carole Lynch, Sligo
Printed by ColourBooks Ltd, Ireland

Contents

Introduction

Senior public servants spend increasing amounts of time managing cross-cutting issues, which require joint working between a number of government departments and agencies. It is clear that these issues are becoming more prominent in public administration generally.

This subject has a real impact in the daily working lives of the authors of this book. Our topic is important not just to the success of the public service today – it is likely to be of increasing significance in the future. It is also the subject of sustained ongoing work and analysis internationally as part of public service reform programmes.

In Ireland, many policy issues that are central to the government's programme such as management of the EU agenda, infrastructure and regional development, social inclusion and immigration management, require integration of effort across government departments for successful management of these issues.

This study examines:

- the treatment of cross-cutting issues in the international literature and in the programme of public service reform in Ireland (Chapter 1)
- environmental factors that drive the management of cross-cutting issues closer to the top of government agendas (Chapter 2)
- policy formulation and implementation challenges in management of cross-cutting issues – with a comparative study of the way these challenges are addressed across several countries (Chapters 3 and 4)
- the challenges that arise for governments in managing the e-government agenda (Chapter 5).

In conclusion, the study gives practical suggestions for improved management of key cross-cutting issues in Ireland across a number of headings based on the best of what we have seen at home and abroad (Chapter 6).

1

Our study encompasses an extensive literature review, a significant interview programme in Ireland, assessment of international best practice based on interviews and analysis in Australia, New Zealand, Singapore, Finland, Denmark and the Netherlands.

It is increasingly apparent that the capacity of countries to manage cross-cutting issues becomes more critical in a volatile global economic and political environment. The countries we studied are focusing increasingly on their own internal capabilities to manage these issues. Critical success factors for the successful management of these issues include the ability to:

- analyse and choose between competing whole-of-government issues
- concentrate resources on effective execution
- enable the political system to lead and support cross-cutting processes
- adapt institutional structures and processes
- influence behaviour across departments and agencies to meet the different requirements of individual departments and cross-cutting activities.

Our review of the way other countries manage cross-cutting issues led us to the following conclusions.

Successful cross-cutting issue management often stems from a long-term emphasis on the importance of policy formulation and policy implementation. Success is less about ad hoc experimentation than a long-term focus on strategic objectives. The countries that do cross-cutting well, do not necessarily do it more, but, rather, do it smarter.

Examples of good cross-cutting work are found where there is a consistent approach between the philosophy of governments/administrations, the long term agenda and short term actions.

Cross-cutting issues are well managed in countries where they are prioritised by the political and administrative systems rather than marginalised on departmental agendas.

Cross-cutting issues are best managed where systems and procedures facilitate ongoing effective dialogue between the political and administrative systems.

Cross-cutting issues are managed better where there is a balance between the leadership role of the centre and the development of appropriate new structures to meet increased demands for public service. In particular, overload at the centre is a clear indication of serious problems in managing cross-cutting issues coherently.

Our recommendations focus on practical and implementable strategies that reflect the impressions we took away from international experience, combined with analysis of the inputs generously given to us by numerous interviewees in the Irish public and private sectors and in the political system. We wish to thank them for their valuable help and support in completing our study.

Reform of Public Administration and the Management of Cross-Cutting Issues

Introduction

During the past two decades, there has been widespread reform and renewal in public sector management internationally. Much of this change has been influenced by the precepts of the New Public Management (NPM) school of thought such as those put forward by Osborne and Gaebler (1992). This model has focused on transforming the traditional public administration into a new form of public management characterised by:

- a separation of strategic policy from operational management
- a concern with results rather than process and procedure
- an orientation to the needs of the citizen rather than the interests of the organisation or the bureaucracy
- a withdrawal from direct service provision in favour of a steering or enabling role
- a changed, entrepreneurial management culture.

Cross-cutting and integration issues in public service reform in Ireland

Many of these NPM principles can be seen in operation in Ireland over recent decades. Despite earlier reviews of systems and structures in the Irish civil service such as the Brennan Commission (1932) and the White Paper on

Economic Development (Fanning, 1978), the first compre-hensive and critical look at the Irish civil service was taken by the Public Services Organisation Review Group (1966–1969), whose report, published in 1969, became known as the Devlin Report. This emerged against the back-ground of a debate beginning in the early 1960s on the need for the public service as a whole to become more involved in national economic planning.

The Devlin Report recommended the separation of the planning and executive functions of departments – the aireacht/executive split – to allow greater emphasis on policy development. It also recognised the need for co-ordination across departments and recommended the establishment of four staff units in each department, i.e. finance, planning, personnel and organisation, as a means of maintaining essential communication throughout the whole of the public service. The Department of Finance was to co-ordinate the planning and finance functions across departments. The new Department of the Public Service (DPS) was to drive the reform process and also to co-ordinate human resource policy in conjunction with the Department of the Taoiseach. Apart from a few exceptions most departments did not espouse the structural reforms. In retrospect, this was hardly surprising. Change was to be imposed from the outside on departments that did not necessarily agree with the need for change, and there was little political support for the reforms. The DPS lasted for some ten years before being subsumed into the Department of Finance. Its final death knell was the economic and fiscal crisis of the late 1980s. Another innovation at that time was the Department of Economic Planning and Development which was established in 1977 to give specific focus to longer term economic planning. It had an even shorter life, largely because the case for separating its functions from those of the Department of Finance had not gained widespread acceptance.

The 1980s

The next attempt at comprehensive reform came in 1985 with the publication of the White Paper *Serving the Country Better* (1985). It addressed concerns about inherent contradictions in the doctrine of ministerial responsibility, by identifying the need for new management systems in departments and emphasising personal responsibility for results, costs and service. Against the backdrop of attempts to introduce a customer service ethos, the management role of the public service was now to be given primacy over the planning role.

The White Paper called for the establishment of management systems and said

- Each department would have an explicit and clear statement of its aims and objectives.
- Specific results to be achieved should be identified in advance and their achievement costed as far as possible.
- Performance should be monitored against plans and budgets.
- The practical contribution of each individual manager should be clearly identified and his or her performance systematically assessed. (p.13)

The White Paper made passing reference to the need for departments, as well as carrying out their own business efficiently, to take a corporate view of their responsibilities as part of the overall public service. The paper quoted from the 11th Report of the Public Service Advisory Council (1985).

> The paradox of the Public Service is that on the one hand it is a unity implementing Government policy and on the other it is an amalgamation of autonomous and semi-autonomous units each seeking a greater allocation of resources and each endeavouring to extend its influence. (p.18)

The White Paper also referred to the possibility, in the increasingly complex world of government, of overlap and duplication of roles but saw the solution to this as the elimination of overlap, after close examination, in the interest of economy and efficiency.

Little progress was made in furthering the White Paper's proposals because from the mid-1980s onwards very difficult economic and fiscal challenges absorbed the attention of the political system and 'public service reform had largely been abandoned by 1987 as a political priority' (Aylward S. et al p.3).

The introduction of the administrative budget system in 1990 partly met the commitment in the White Paper to greater delegation of responsibility to line departments and, in many respects, it heralded the next phase in the reform agenda.

1990s – The Strategic Management Initiative (SMI)

Murray (2001, p. 4) described the specific context out of which the SMI reforms were born as follows:

> .... the origins of SMI are both robust and challenging. They are robust in so far as lessons of the past and dangers of the present appear to have been absorbed into its formulation and implementation. They are challenging in so far as they opened up many difficult issues for discussion and decision. The latter are now the main inheritance of the initiative and how it evolves to deal with them will be pivotal.

A defining characteristic of this new approach to public service reform was that it was intended to be both 'top down' and 'bottom up' in approach. It was 'top down' in approach in the sense that renewal was to be undertaken by encouraging departments and offices to apply the principles of strategic management in accordance with an initiative which was to be driven centrally by the Department of the Taoiseach. It was 'bottom up' in the sense that each department and office was to develop its own plan, within certain parameters, to maximise its efficiency and effectiveness.

The achievement of better co-ordination of activities across departments was seen as one of the major potential benefits of the Strategic Management Initiative as was made clear by the then Secretary General, Department of the Taoiseach:

> ... an important strength of the initiative is the contribution it makes to the identification and thus more effective management of key issues across departments which can only be addressed in a global context. Certain trans-departmental issues may involve only a few departments, while others may be almost universal. Examples of trans-departmental issues are: social services, including child care; job creation and competitiveness; and infrastructural development, including environmental protection. As you can see, this is a very diverse and complex area, involving a web of causal connections which only a cohesive strategy for the public service as a whole can hope to manage and co-ordinate to best effect. (Teahon, 1996)

By late 1994, most departments and offices had submitted their first strategy statement to the Co-ordinating Group of Secretaries. In commenting on the first statements of strategy, the co-ordinating group noted that progress had been made in establishing a strategic management process, although much remained to be done including, among other things, the creation of inter-departmental synergies.

Boyle and Fleming (2000) found significant improvements in the quality of statements overall from 1996 to 1998. However, in a discussion of the content of strategy statements, they identified significant limitations in many statements and found scope for improvements in future iterations. Among the issues identified were poor environmental analysis and a tendency to list cross-departmental issues rather than set out how to secure better co-ordination. (p. 31 ff.)

As a next step in the process the Co-ordinating Group established interdepartmental committees of assistant secretaries to review and propose changes in personnel and financial management practices and cross-departmental issues, while also taking account of the results of research on reforms in the New Zealand and Australian public services.

In March 1995 the government requested the group to:

- Review existing systems for making decisions, allocating responsibility and ensuring accountability in the Irish Civil service; and
- Bring forward for Government consideration, proposals for an integrated programme to modernise the systems and practices in question and for the consequent modernisation of existing personnel and financial management in the Civil Service (p. 1).

Delivering Better Government – 1996

In response, the Co-ordinating Group published *Delivering Better Government* (DBG) in 1996. The key objective of the report was 'the achievement of an excellent service for the Government and for the public'. DBG identified two aspects to service provision – firstly, the social aspect (i.e. the well-being of the citizen and the coherence of society); and secondly, the economic aspects (the importance for national competitiveness of the work of the civil service).

The report set out a vision for the civil service based on the following six key areas:

- a framework for change emphasising, in particular, a customer orientation, results orientation and embedding of a strategic management process at the heart of departments
- delivery of quality services
- high-quality policy advice for government
- reduction of red-tape and regulatory reform
- open and transparent service delivery
- managing cross-departmental issues.

Achieving the vision would require a new management structure, and new approaches to human resource management, a fully integrated performance management process, a new finance management system and effective use of information technology.

The report highlighted concerns about the management of cross-departmental issues, both in relation to the provision of policy advice and in the delivery of services. With a view to achieving better co-ordination it recommended the development and implementation of strategic result areas and the delivery of an integrated quality service. Strategic result areas were defined as key priority areas of government activity, consistent with the government programme, e.g. eliminating poverty, tackling crime and improving competitiveness, with required outcomes specified over given time periods.

The Co-ordinating Group of Secretaries noted that these new approaches challenge traditional departmental and functional boundaries. Quarterly meetings of all secretaries and heads of office were proposed to discuss critical issues and to facilitate communication. Finally, active dialogue and consultation within the civil service was recommended, involving departmental staff in a partnership process and consultation with the Irish Congress of Trade Unions (ICTU) and the civil service unions.

In relation to the policymaking process, there has undoubtedly been significant improvement in the way in which policy is formulated since the publication of DBG in 1996. Much of the landscape for addressing cross-departmental policy making has changed significantly since the publication of DBG in 1996. The Public Service Management Act 1997, the development of the cabinet committee system, the more collaborative approach to policymaking and the use of cross-departmental teams have together created a much different context and environment for dealing with these issues.

Delivering Better Government and management of cross-cutting issues

It is worth dwelling further on the concerns expressed in *Delivering Better Government* (1996) about the management of cross-cutting issues.

During the 1990s there had been an upsurge in the level

of interdepartmental activity and a growing recognition of the interdependence of different policy areas. The development of mechanisms to deal with them had been largely ad hoc and involved interdepartmental committees, more broadly-based committees and task forces, working groups, advisory groups, commissions etc.

In some cases, new government departments were set up to co-ordinate difficult cross-cutting policy issues such as equality. In other cases, such as the area of child care, a minister of state was given specific responsibility and was appointed to a number of different departments in order to achieve a better level of co-operation and co-ordination. In yet other cases, one government department was given a lead role in pulling together a policy issue involving a number of other departments, e.g. the then Department of Social Welfare was given such a role in the development of proposals for an integrated social services system. There was also a tendency for the lead responsibility on difficult issues to be pulled to the centre and for central departments to be given, in effect, the lead role in the development of policy in certain cases.

Delivering Better Government (1996) expressed concerns that the existing civil service structure was not well adapted to deal with areas where cross-departmental commitment and expertise was required. It observed that each department's work is firmly focused on a sectoral and functional basis, with limited structures for consultations and co-ordination, and a system that rewards territorial protection (DBG, 1996, p.14) at the expense of active co-operation to achieve results.

DBG recommended the development of strategic result areas as a means by which individual organisations would focus, in a coherent, consistent and co-ordinated way, on achieving the objectives of government and on contributing to the overall implementation of policy. In short, 'a shared agenda will be developed for Departments and Offices' (1996, p.10).

Cabinet sub-committees and strategic result areas

DBG recommended the establishment of cabinet sub-committees for key areas of government policy, the allocation of specific co-ordination roles to ministers and ministers of state, the systematic sharing of expertise between departments, and the nomination of lead departments in areas to ensure action is taken and the required outputs obtained.

It went on to say that pending the development of strategic result areas and in order to assist in the process, cross-departmental teams should be established with co-ordination assigned to a minister/minister of state and with a specific lead department. Areas identified which would benefit immediately were: drugs, employment, competitiveness, unemployment and social exclusion, financial services, local development and island development.

DBG recommended that these teams be given a specific remit and detailed objectives over an agreed period. Team members would be detached from their departments on a full or part time basis by reference to the specific skills they would bring to resolving issues within the team framework. A clear obligation would be placed on the team to develop solutions and new approaches. Suitable reward mechanisms would need to be designed for this work. Summer 1996 was set as the target date to set up pilot teams. The lessons learned and the 'best practice' emerging could then be identified and utilised to introduce systematic and innovative process for addressing key issues of national importance and to assist in the development of strategic results areas.

While DBG is the most recent milestone in this historical overview of public service reform in Ireland, it is also appropriate to mention three further reform initiatives which stem from it but are important in their own right.

The first was the launch, in May 1997, of a Quality Customer Service (QCS) Initiative to promote the wider adoption of improved customer service standards by twenty-three departments/offices.

The second most recent initiative was the launch, in May 2000, of a new Performance Management and Development

System (PMDS), as part of a new human resource strategy which is currently being finalised.

The third initiative is the development of a Management Information Framework (MIF), work on the overall design of which was completed in late 2001. DBG (1996) was concerned with achieving value for money and ensuring that available resources were targeted to areas of greatest need. Meeting this requirement implied enhancement of information systems within the civil service to monitor resource allocation, prioritise the resources so allocated, and measure the value for money secured from spending programmes.

MIF represents a critical element in the wider DBG context. The full and successful application of the MIF will be necessary if departments/offices are to engage in any meaningful way with issues such as the quantification and measurement of service outputs, performance management, value for money, business planning, resource allocation, resource consumption, and financial reports. Few, if any, of these areas will be successfully progressed in the absence of a fully operational MIF.

These three initiatives are significant because they have the potential to become, in time, important tools in the management of cross-cutting issues. The QCS initiative may have a role to play in tackling the lack of effective co-ordination, which is probably one of the most commonly heard complaints about public service delivery (Boyle, 1999, p.75). The PMDS, by linking into departmental business and strategy formulation processes, can facilitate the development of cross-departmental skills and competencies. Equally, a fully operational MIF could contribute effectively to financing and evaluation methodologies for cross-departmental initiatives.

As a result of the DBG report, the Public Service Management Act was enacted in 1997 to provide the framework to enable the public service to respond to the demands of a more complex society and to address issues on a whole-of-government basis. It provides for devolution of functions in relation to the management of departments from ministers to secretaries general. The intention of the Act is to provide for a new management structure to enhance the management, effectiveness and transparency of the work of departments. It also provides for the mechanisms to be put in place to address, develop and implement proposals in respect of issues that cross the remit of a number of departments or agencies. However, this provision has been relatively little used by the public service. There are no incentives within or across port-folios for including cross-cutting issues within budgets; neither are there processes for managing and prioritising cross-portfolio issues between departments and agencies.

This view is supported by a review of strategy statements (Boyle et al, 2000) which found that very little attention has been paid to explicitly recognising and analysing the role of individual departments in cross cutting-issues and there has not yet been an example where departments have come together in the context of the Strategy Statements to devise a way forward collaboratively. In effect, the 'as is' seems to be taken as a given and the opportunity to think in a more corporate, evolving way has not been taken up.

Evaluation of progress

It is not the purpose of this study to undertake a detailed evaluation of progress on the reform agenda in Ireland. That task has been addressed in the recently published report by the PA Consulting Group (PA, 2002). The report contains the most authoritative assessment to date of the modernisation programme in Ireland and includes a detailed evaluation of what has been achieved since the publication of *Delivering Better Government* in 1996.

There has been undoubted progress in many cross-cutting areas: strategically, through national level strategies such as the NAPS; specifically on co-ordination frameworks under ministers of state, such as the National Children's Office and the forthcoming Social Inclusion Office; on project level, with teams such as the National Drugs Task Force, the Cross-Departmental team on Housing, the Cross-Agency Team on the Homeless.

The PA Consulting Group's evaluation of SMI (2002) is a comprehensive treatment of the subject and its conclusions are generally positive in relation to progress made. Their overall conclusion was that

> ... the civil service in 2002 is a more effective organisation than it was a decade ago. Much of this change can be attributed to SMI/DBG. However, the implementation of the modernisation programme is not yet complete. (2002, p. 1)

The report went on to recommend that the Implementation Group of Secretaries General working with a renewed strong mandate from government must develop and present a vision of the civil service to 2007. It identified the 'challenge of implementation' (p.7) as the key theme to emerge from the SMI/DBG programme. It also identified the failure to develop adequate mechanisms for tackling cross-departmental or cross-cutting issues.

Accepting that the challenge of implementation is a key issue, it is worth exploring what are the implementation deficits in relation to cross-cutting issues. Murray assesses progress on cross-departmental issues in the following terms:

> The fifth element of the framework [cross-cutting] presents a ... puzzle. There have been considerable advances in the creation and effective use of a variety of 'cross-cutting' mechanisms to deal with important national issues in an integrated manner. Much remains to be done, but achievement is noteworthy. The organisational mechanisms that have been deployed may be seen as overlays on the traditional hierarchical and segmented structures of the civil service. The latter inherently destroy integration and promote confusion, contradiction, increased costs and ineffectiveness in matters that cannot be properly corralled within one departmental remit. DBG notes forcefully that matters which cannot be corralled in this manner are often the most important matters of state. While increasing achievement on managing cross-cutting issues must be

applauded, it is not clear quite what happens next. Should the mechanisms now in use become a permanent repertoire? Or are such overlays just temporary means of overcoming rigidities in underlying structure that must ultimately be attacked directly and re-created? (Murray 2001, p.12)

Commenting on the lack of progress in tackling cross-cutting issues, the PA Consulting Group (2002) recommended as follows:

Cross-cutting issues have been a central concern of SMI/DBG. In respect of some notable policy areas (such as child welfare) new cross-cutting structures have been established and appear to be working well. In relation to more routine instances of over-lapping concerns across Departments/Offices we have seen less evidence of effective collaboration arrangements. In terms of moving forward, this aspect of cross-departmental collaboration will require further attention if the treatment of cross cutting issues is to conform with the expectations of DBG. Equally, appropriate reward structures will be required to support this development. (PA, 2002, p. 96)

What is New Public Management reform?

Returning to the question of how Ireland stands internationally in relation to the renewal agenda, Murray (2001) considers that placing the Irish reforms in an international context:

.... reveals that the SMI has been of a piece with the generality of reform. It aligns with the practice of modernizer states, typically North European, with a strong reform agenda, radicalism tempered by consensus building and a desire for no more than minimal government. In aspiration at least, it might be positioned at the more active and comprehensive boundary of this cluster of countries and reform movements (Murray, 2001 p. 10).

Most academic writers, such as Pollitt and Bouckaert (2000, p.17), describe 'reform' as 'deliberate changes to the structures and processes of public sector organisations with the objective of getting them (in some sense) to perform better'. The changes are coherent and purposive, taking place over a limited time and resulting in a change from an unreformed to a reformed state. But a recent OECD (2001) consultation paper suggests that there is no coherent set of reform theories encompassing the changes which have taken place in public administration in the countries it surveyed between 1991 and 2001. Change, it suggests, has been prompted by a mixture of societal changes, governance changes (how the societies constitute themselves) and planned and unplanned management changes, some deliberately introduced and some ad hoc.

Examining the reform processes in ten OECD member states and the European Commission, Pollitt and Bouckaert (2000) suggest that there are clusters of countries, reflecting how each has pursued reform. Each politico administrative system shapes the approach to, implementation of, and appetite for reform. Anglo-Saxon countries such as Australia, Canada, New Zealand and the UK, they believe 'are much more open to the 'performance driven' market-favouring ideas of the NPM than the others' (Pollitt and Bouckaert, 2000, p. 60). Germany and France are interested in reform but resistant to NPM ideas. By contrast, Nordic countries, such as Finland, the Netherlands and Sweden have displayed 'a general disposition towards consensual, often meso-corporatist styles of governance...(and)...a cautious rather than a wildly enthusiastic approach to ... privatisation' (Pollitt and Bouckaert, 2000, p.61)

Divergence of outcomes from intentions in reform process

No reform theory – however pure – can be put into practice in an undiluted form. As Pollitt and Bouckaert (2000) note, there are constraints on international public management reforms. Reformers often censor their own proposals in the hope of framing a package with a better chance of being accepted.

In addition, reform schemes are rarely comprehensive, even in intent. Even where (as in New Zealand) reforms are characterised by both theoretical coherence and internal consistency and are driven by one key driver (in the case of New Zealand, both the Ministry of Finance and the State Services Commission), reforms still tend to evolve over time and be influenced by practical considerations. The *force majeure* of politics inevitably blunts the purity of the underlying theories.

A further complication, as Pollitt and Bouckaert (2000) note, arises from internal inconsistencies in reform programmes. For example, reforms designed to make savings, especially top-down limits on overall spending, often conflict with those designed for performance improvement, because opportunistic cuts may create an unpredictable and negative environment for operational managers, who find they lose part of their budget for no good performance-related reason.

Implementation of reform can take a considerable time. Schick (2001) makes this point and, in this context, eight years of SMI-type renewal is not unduly long. It is also sometimes forgotten that managing a process of change in a large, complex private sector organisation can also take considerable time. Doz and Prahalad (1987) reported that multi-national corporations took between three and ten years to accomplish strategic redirection. This is because, as Pettigrew (1985) found in his study of ICI, large organisations contain massive forces for inertia in structures, systems and political processes. Schick (2001), writing of New Zealand, also emphasises the importance of 'institutionalising' change before moving on to the next stage.

The results of reform plans are also vulnerable to a variety of politico-administrative roadblocks and unforeseen developments of all kinds. Other constraints identified by Pollitt and Bouckaert (2000) include constitutional arrangements and administrative factors such as the costs of new IT and accounting systems. Perhaps as a safeguard against this phenomenon, many of the changes mooted in Delivering

Better Government have been underpinned with legislation or administrative codes. The Public Service Management Act 1997, the Freedom of Information Act 1997 and the Principles of Quality Customer Service are but three examples.

Public service reform and cross-cutting issues

The widespread application of New Public Management precepts poses a number of crucial questions in the treatment of cross-cutting issues. These include the role of the centre – is it the guardian of probity, the overall motor and moulder of policy or a super-referee arbitrating between competing interests?

One of the characteristic aspects of NPM reform is the separation of purchase from provision. In public sector reform as pursued in Ireland (as in several of the countries visited for this study) there has been increased resort to 'agentisation'. While there are undoubted merits to a policy of agentisation *per se*, it also poses problems of co-ordination. It requires clear definition of roles – including that of the agency itself, the centre and the relationship between the two. This issue is explored in greater detail in Chapters 3 and 4.

Sabel and O'Donnell (2000) have asserted that the results of New Public Management in public sector reform are at best equivocal, and that in the UK, in particular, government is less accountable and on balance no more effective than before. This is because of the difficulty of separating strategy from implementation, and the fact that narrowing programmes in the interest of accountability makes it difficult to co-ordinate the narrower entities. Local clarity was achieved but there was nothing to induce agencies to co-operate among themselves to solve problems requiring their joint action. Recognition of these difficulties has led to significant recent analysis in the UK on cross-cutting problems (UK Cabinet Office, 2000).

Recognition of these difficulties is not confined to the UK. A report to the New Zealand Government in November 2001(Review of the Centre, 2001, p.15) acknowledges that 'the fragmentation of the State sector… (due to) … the large number of agencies, portfolios and votes, makes it more difficult to agree and actively pursue cross-cutting objectives, and provide integrated service delivery'.

The Review of the Centre Report (2001) also acknowledges the tendency for aspects of the system to reinforce co-ordination problems by allowing or encouraging people to ignore wider government interests. This report records that, while structural changes which led to the large number of agencies have provided benefits in terms of sharper focus and avoiding conflicting functions, the narrow focus of organisations can inhibit seeing whole-of-government connections and make it difficult to get enough high calibre people to govern and manage the large number of agencies.

The report's planned initiatives to address fragmentation and improve alignment of state sector agencies include the establishment of a network of related agencies to better integrate policy, delivery and capability-building in the state sector, and a process of structural consolidation. The report also recommends that organisations at the centre should exert more effective leadership across the wider state sector by formally adopting as part of their core business a respon-sibility to lead on whole-of-government initiatives. This is discussed further in Chapter 4.

Pollitt and Bouckaert (2000) note that, all things being equal, increasing specialisation usually results in greater autonomy for individual service delivery organisations. But, as has been argued by Greiner (1998), in a private sector business context, the solution to a current cycle of problems can often sow the seed of future problems in the next cycle of an organisation's evolution. Increasing specialisation implies a need for greater co-ordination if the level of over-all coherence of policy and services is to be maintained. Pollitt and Bouckaert (2000) found persuasive evidence of a trade off between increased levels of institutional autonomy and some loss of policy or programme co-ordination. This was borne out in the countries we visited when collecting material for this study.

In Ireland also, a study by Boyle et al (2002) found that frag-mentation of departments and offices into units, originally put in place to deal with specific issues, makes responsibility for addressing longer term cross-cutting policy issues no-one's responsibility. It is crucial that this issue be addressed.

The cross-cutting challenge for public administration today

Traditionally, co-ordination was achieved through the hierarchy which imposed regulation from the centre. It can also be achieved through voluntary co-operation within a network. (This is more easily achieved when objectives are widely shared, communications are simple and effective, and the scale of operations is modest). A third mode, which was the main thrust of NPM reforms, is that hierarchy should be replaced by the market mechanism, whereby the 'hidden hand', as Pollitt and Bouckaert (2000 p. 80) describe it, of supply and demand co-ordinates activities, assisted by modern ICT.

A study (Perri 6, 1999) of the direction of public sector management in Britain since the late 1990s, found that the reforms of the 1980s and early 1990s focused on the efficient delivery of specific activities. However, it was realised that efficiency gains were bought at a high price, and exacerbated deep-rooted problems of lack of co-ordination. Agencies were trying to manage budgets rather than tackle problems and the lack of co-ordination created waste and incoherence at every level. The importance of holistic working, integration, co-ordination, and joint managerial arrangements is now widely recognised.

The action needed is not rocket science, as the authors point out. It includes a broad spectrum, from dialogue and consultation through to large-scale reorganisation and merger. This demands strategic focus, rather than skills which are new or fundamentally different from those that good public managers already possess. However, pooled budgets, co-located staff, one-stop-shops, integrated electronic consumer information systems and so on, on their own, are neither necessary nor sufficient to achieve holistic working. They are valuable only in the context of integrated accountability and knowledge. And crucially, the authors suggest, holistic working cannot be imposed from the centre but must grow out from every level of government.

Hence, the proper management of cross cutting-issues involves much more than mere co-ordination. It may require entirely new types of behaviour, new structures, different budgetary procedures, and new ways of working. All of these elements are explored in detail in Chapters 3 and 4.

However, organisational integration can also lead to increased administrative costs, as pointed out by Hill and Jones (2001). It is clear that the higher the level of differentiation, the higher is the level of integration needed. In today's increasingly complex world, as pointed out by Lawrence and Dyer (1983), 'information complexity' requires increasing organisational differentiation, which in turn requires increasing integration to give the essential co-ordination. There are organisational costs in both, and an inappropriate mix of high integration and low differentiation means over-control with loss of flexibility and speed. It is therefore necessary to achieve the right balance of integration and differentiation.

Problem solving on a cross-cutting issue often involves the need to develop a capacity for innovation and creativity. In this context, Kanter (1983) recommends 'integrative thinking' which is more likely to occur where cultures and structures are also integrative and treat problems as 'wholes'. Integrative organisations reduce conflict and isolation between organisational units. They create mechanisms for exchange of information. Multiple perspectives are taken into account in decision making and provide coherence and direction to the whole organisation. A segmentalist approach militates against this integrative process. Segments work independently and there is no mechanism for the transfer of knowledge from one segment to another. Communication between segments is often problematic because it is confined to 'good news'. The acknowledgement of the existence of a problem is perceived as a failure (which brings more work for the identifier – a disincentive for action). Furthermore, in a segmented organisation specialisation in career paths leaves no inducement for co-operation.

An integrative approach to problem solving is key to the management of cross-cutting issues. In considering how this approach might be achieved, Kanter notes that supportive peers and horizontal co-operation are essential. Furthermore, a sense of unity or identification with the whole cannot be imposed, but must derive from the way the work is done.

Kanter suggests that integrating devices might include:

- employment security, which generates longer-term thinking and safety in tackling projects that may not guarantee short-term results
- frequent mobility, including lateral moves
- extensive use of formal team mechanisms which are best drawn from diverse sources to create a 'market place of ideas' rather than the 'caution of committees' or group-think
- complex ties permitting cross-cutting access.

In matrixed organisations there are direct reporting and 'dotted-line' relationships that give legitimate access to support, resources and information.

Kanter further argues that integrative systems have an advantage in strategy formulation because they promote open thinking and wider circulation of ideas. Teams at the top draw many areas together and exchange ideas. Pre-existing coalitions and co-operative traditions work to facilitate action and decision making.

In a comparison with Kanter's recommendations, the Irish civil service scores highly on the employment security scale, although it is questionable whether the predicted benefits of longer-term thinking have materialised. Kanter's suggestions on mobility and teamwork are part of developing human resources policies in promoting the ability to operate across silos. Finally, while reporting relationships do not tend to cut across hierarchies, there are close working relationships in Ireland especially at senior level that do facilitate cross-cutting access.

In relation to integration, the Irish civil service has made significant use of informal integrating mechanisms such as task forces, teams and inter-departmental liaison roles. More use could be made of shared information systems which can also act as an effective integrating mechanism. Departmental systems frequently cannot communicate with each other and, even where there are shared departmental databases, the time and skills necessary for their full development is frequently lacking.

Conclusion

Public service reform in Ireland, and SMI/DBG in particular, have helped to bring about a more effective civil service. DBG identified the management of cross-cutting issues as one of six key areas of its vision for the civil service. However, apart from one or two policy areas, there has been a failure to develop adequate mechanisms for tackling cross-departmental issues. This is a matter which will require further attention if the expectations of DBG are to be realised.

Academic literature on public sector management and reform contains surprisingly little on the topic of cross-cutting issues *per se*. Furthermore, although cross-cutting issues are arguably just as important for the countries visited by us, there was little systematic evaluation as to whether or not they were dealt with successfully, and no common vocabulary or models for dealing with them.

In part this may be due to the fact that in Ireland and inter-nationally this has been an aspect of the reform agenda most difficult to resolve, where neither modest successes, nor even current failures, are fully documented.

The environmental analysis in Chapter 2 of this book suggests that this is a situation which requires continuous atten-tion in an increasingly complex, volatile and economically-connected world. Recent reviews of the progress of public service reform by the OECD have clearly pointed to the need for coherence and integration as one of the primary challenges facing administrations at the start of the twenty-first century. The analysis in this chapter supports the view of the OECD, that there are clear gaps between the need for coherence and the capacity of most administrations to achieve it. Furthermore, there is no evidence of the existence of a single policy making system which guarantees improved coherence. There are however good practices and tools of coherence; it is to these and the structures, arrangements, HRM and financial practices in place in the countries we studied that we turn in the following chapters.

In other chapters we will look at policy and implementation aspects of cross-cutting issues, focus in particular on the example of e-government as a cross-cutting issue in itself, and put forward some new issues for discussion and proposals for consideration under the next phase of the modernisation programme.

2

The External Environment and Cross-Cutting Issues

Introduction

The scale of the political, economic and social change which has occurred in recent decades in the OECD has been profound. These changes, together with new emerging challenges, will ultimately determine the agenda for government and public management.

One of the leading challenges for public management revolves around the initiation and management of change in the most efficient and effective manner (OECD, 2000). Most aspects of public administration are handled within well-established departmental and local structures. Administrative systems are normally well-established within a single organisation which are likely to operate relatively efficiently. There are, however, an increasing number of issues within public administration which do not neatly fit within existing governmental and departmental administrative structures.

Why adopt a cross-cutting approach?

There are a number of different models which may be used to put in place a more efficient and co-ordinated administrative response to manage issues of common interest to a number of government departments. These different models will be examined in more detail in later chapters. But for the moment, it is necessary to acknowledge that the use of formal cross-cutting structures and processes generally takes place because, at some basic level, the perceived benefits obtained from these integration structures and processes exceeds their costs and the alternative, ignoring the need for closer integration of departmental strategies and policies or establishing new agencies to deal with cross-cutting issues, is not practical.

Typically, the immediate costs for public policymakers of managing cross-cutting issues include transaction costs – the resources allocated to managing and operating cross-cutting processes, and indirect costs imposed by system changes required for cross-cutting processes.

Less obvious but nevertheless important costs include increased potential for political and administrative conflict within the public service, and potential for reduced control and personal/political accountability around some of the issues which are part of the cross-cutting process.

Examples of issues now managed on a cross-cutting basis

As indicated in the previous chapter, cross-cutting issues have become more important in Irish public administration, particularly over the past 10-15 years. Over the past decade, a judgement has been made, either explicitly or implicitly, that the benefits of dealing with a number of issues in a cross-cutting way exceed the costs. This is illustrated by the following examples:

Management of EU Issues – optimising Irish negotiating strategy across a range of portfolios at EU level and dealing with critical issues such as structural funding and enlargement

Regional development – focused on minimising income and economic development disparities across the regions

Public infrastructure – centred on the capability and com-petitiveness of physical infrastructure in the state

E-government – the rollout of public services to all citizens on a variety of electronic and information technology media.

Sectoral regulation – including resource management, technical and political interface issues

Poverty management – focused on cross-departmental approaches to eliminating poverty and the problems created by social and economic disadvantage in Irish society

The drugs issue – dealing with a need to reduce both supply of and demand for illegal drugs as well as focussing on public services available to those affected by the problem

Environmental protection – addressing the interface between environment protection and the policies impacting on the environment as implemented by a wide variety of government departments and agencies

Research – dealing with the imperative of moving Irish industrial activity in many sectors up the value chain

Equality – aimed at developing an inclusive and egalitarian society.

All of these issues are cross-cutting. They are not confined to the area of responsibility of a single government department or agency and responsibility for their execution depends on a number of departments and agencies working effectively and co-operatively together. Chapters 3 and 4 below will focus on the need to put in place specific structures and mechanisms in managing these issues on a cross-cutting basis.

Features emerging

On reviewing the range of cross-cutting issues outlined above, the following conclusions appear valid. The number/ prevalence of the cross-cutting issues which are or should be handled on a cross-cutting basis in Irish public administration is increasing. The political and administrative importance of these issues relative to issues handled exclusively within departmental 'silos' is increasing. These are long term issues – there is no indication that the issues being handled on a cross-cutting basis by departments are due to disappear in the short to medium term – in fact this chapter will argue that there is every evidence to suggest that they will continue to move up the government priority list.

Our perspective on the future

Against this analysis of the recent past and paying particular attention to the work of the OECD's Public Management Service (PUMA), an assessment of the major factors which will shape the environment for the next five to ten years and possibly beyond suggests that five major areas will be key:

- *Ireland's changing political relationship with the world*, particularly in the context of an enlarged EU
- the *external economic environment and the challenge of maintaining competitiveness* in an era of increasing globalisation
- *technological change*
- *societal change*, involving changes in value systems and influenced by changing demographics and immigration patterns
- the *fiscal situation*, linked to the need to adhere to the EU's Stability and Growth Pact, which will help determine the resources which are available to the government to meet the various demands upon it.

For each of these areas, this chapter briefly reviews the Irish experience and then attempts to predict the future changes which are in prospect. When the future perspectives for each of these areas are assembled, the composite picture represents our best guess of what we believe the main outlines of the future will look like. This composite picture will help define the main challenges faced by the Irish system of public administration. It is also this picture which we argue will lead to more integrated government in the future.

Ireland's political relationship with the external world

Ireland's entry in 1973 to the European Economic Community, later to become the European Union (EU), marked a fundamental change in its relationship with the external world. Entry represented a commitment to work towards a shared sovereignty on a path of political and economic integration. Over the intervening years, membership of the EU has had a profound impact on Irish political and administrative life. Seeking to advance national objectives within the EU decision-making framework has required working closely with the European Commission and the building of coalitions with other member states. It has also required significant co-ordination and co-operation between Irish bodies at home.

The forthcoming enlargement of the EU represents a major challenge for the existing institutions and for the decision-making processes both in the EU and in Ireland. The implications of these changes are profound for the Irish political and administrative system. With more complex decision making, the need for successful coalition building in order to achieve national objectives becomes more challenging. As a successful economy, the financial, policy and regulatory environment within which Ireland must operate is becoming far more complex.

The emerging EU context within which policy is decided and implemented has some significant implications for the civil service. Laffan (2001) has identified three phases of the EU policy process, namely, agenda setting, the negotiating phase and the implementation phase. She postulates that, heretofore, Ireland has tended to focus more on the negotiating stage at Council level and not sufficiently on the other two phases. She further asserts that Ireland's approach to coordination has not been sufficiently collegiate, strategic or agenda driven.

In an enlarged EU, there will be a growing need to make bilateral contacts with the key players in order to be in the information loop from the start of the process. The Irish Presidency in 2004 represents a major challenge, requiring a more structured level of integration than ever before.

At an international level there are issues on which Ireland, by virtue of its relative prosperity and aspirations to implement a progressive foreign policy, may wish to play a more active role. Global environment and sustainable development issues come within this category. Any ambitions to play such an active role will have implications for the vision and skills of individual civil servants. Because many of these issues are cross-cutting, they also have implications for the coordination mechanisms to handle these issues.

The external economic environment

The past

EU membership has had a profound effect on Ireland's economic performance over the past three decades (ESRI, 2001) although there have been considerable variations in the level of performance over that period. While the low growth levels of the 1980s were influenced by a number of global factors and a sluggish growth performance at European level, most commentators would agree that poor domestic policy choices in the late 1970s and 1980s were also responsible. The economic successes of the 1990s were due to a combination of factors. These included the completion of the EU's single market and a number of long-term domestic policies (e.g. education, industrial and taxation policy), which bore fruit during the decade. Effective social partnership from 1987 onwards is also seen to have played an important role in the economic success of the 1990s.

The future

Looking to the future, the recent ESRI medium term review (2001) highlighted the fact that the exceptionally high rate of economic growth of the past five years has meant that Ireland has not fully adjusted to its position as one of the wealthiest countries in the world. The ESRI's analysis goes on to argue that while, in the past, the economic priority was to increase growth in GNP to deal with the problem of unemployment, the advent of near full employment may change priorities. These changed priorities may include increased focus on poverty alleviation, on family friendly policies and on leisure and quality of life issues – all of which are cross-cutting issues.

Safeguarding competitiveness

If such a shift in priorities and attitudes does occur, a key cross-cutting question will be how the competitiveness of the Irish economy can be protected. During the 1990s Ireland's economic competitiveness increased and underpinned the increase in national output and employment. A wide range of measures of competitiveness is available. There is much debate as to the conceptual frameworks used and indeed the data. However on almost all international comparative competitiveness indices, Ireland moved sharply upwards during the 1990s.

The sheer pace of income growth in Ireland over the past decade has brought to the fore the problem of economic management of transition. The shift from one phase of development to the next typically requires new ways of organising government, markets and economic sectors. Many countries fail to make the transition or even fail to understand that it is required if growth is to be maintained. In 2000-2001, in terms of the overall Global Competitiveness Index (World Economic Forum, 2001), Ireland's ranking fell from 4 to 11 in just one year. This significant fall in relative competitiveness could be mainly attributed to the challenge for Ireland in moving from a resource-based economy up the value chain to a knowledge-based economy. Ireland's challenge in global competitiveness terms is to justify higher wage levels and higher local costs without yet having developed a world-class innovative structure. This will not be possible without very clear strategic thinking and execution across the public sector. Chapters 3 and 4 will show that the capacity to make the transition to higher levels of economic development requires effective management of the cross-issues which form part of this process.

Technology

Technology is often referred to as a key driver of economic and societal change (Michalski, 1999). We are concerned with the extent to which technology development is changing *the content* of public policy, *the context* of public policy and *the way* in which public services and public administration are organised and managed. Technology and governance require a form of co-evolution which allows technological development to co-exist with significant diffusion of government authority and responsibility.

Three aspects of technology change have particular relevance to these organisational issues.

The rate of technology change: how fast is technology changing? Clearly, the faster the pace, the more difficult it is for single government agencies to respond appropriately to the challenges involved. Examples of areas where pace of change has created governance difficulties include information and communications technology and, internationally, genetics and biotechnology.

The rate at which the technology change is seen on the market: even if the pace of technology change is very challenging, the pace at which change is brought to the market is possibly the ultimate arbiter of the scale of the governance challenge in the public sector. The combination of finance and technology is a particularly tough one for government to manage effectively. This can often create a demand for new institutional arrangements to manage public policy in areas where a high level of technological expertise or understanding is required. For example, the need to license new forms of communications technology has been a challenging issue for governments globally over the past five to ten years.

Complexity/difficulty of governance around these technology changes: ultimately the combination of the pace and nature of technology change and the time to market issue dictates the scale of the governance issue for the policymaker. In addition, the existence of an economic imperative to 'climb the value chain' creates a policy drive to foster and embrace technology change to support this over-riding objective. The operation of global financial markets and competitive markets creates a framework in which technology development is increasingly imposing new institutional demands on many aspects of public policy.

Societal change

The scale of change in Irish society over the past decade has been profound. That change has had an enormous impact on the environment for public management in the economy.

In general terms, Ireland has become-

- *more diverse* – a more heterogeneous culture produces a more fast moving and volatile environment within which government seeks to deliver public services to the citizen
- *more mobile* – the mobility of human and financial resources places new demands on effectiveness of public policies and public agencies
- *more fragmented* – cultural, economic and social forces produce a citizenry that is not just diverse but has a variety of fundamentally different outlooks, requirements and expectations of government and the public service
- *more affluent* – economic growth produces a population which is better informed, more economically active and interested and, in relation to public service, more concerned with accountability
- *more secular* – the values and ethos of a more secular society help create an environment in which the demands placed on government and public services are more demanding and diverse than in the past
- *more educated* – combined with affluence, higher levels of education produce a population with an active, demanding, diverse and informed series of expectations
- *older* – a rising age profile can lead to new and more demanding levels of engagement between the public and the public service provider
- *more interdependent* – a high level of economic interdependence requires more effective management regimes in both public and private sectors; interdependence also increases a society's exposure to economic risk
- *more open* – an economy which operates increasingly within a global marketplace makes rising demands in terms of the cost-competitiveness of public services and basic infrastructure
- *more competitive* – becomes the defining driver of important elements of public policy in a small open

economy driven mainly, but not solely, by a process of globalisation
- *more technology driven* – producing a society where attitudes to, access to and treatment of information is increasingly driven by technology rather than tradition.

What is required of public service in Ireland is clearly increasingly complex and will require integrated action across government to devise and deliver appropriate policies, with many of the key questions resolvable only through a successful cross-cutting approach.

Looking to the future, a number of important factors will contribute to further societal change over the next decade. Two are worth focussing on specifically – demographic ageing and immigration – because each of them will pose significant political and administrative challenges which will require a cross-cutting approach.

Demographic ageing

The demographic characteristics of OECD and many non-OECD countries have changed considerably compared with a few decades ago (Visco, 2001). Since the post-war baby boom, fertility rates have declined from the end of the 1960s, to levels which in almost all OECD countries are now at or below the 2.1 children required to maintain a stable population. Throughout the same period, improvements in living standards, health care and nutrition have led to an increase in life expectancy. Over the next five decades fertility in the OECD will remain below the rate required to stabilise the population and life expectancy is expected to increase further. Together, these trends will substantially modify the demography of countries towards an older and declining working age population. The old age dependency ratio – the number of people over 65 years relative to the number aged between 20 and 64 – in the OECD area could more than double, to reach nearly 50 per cent in 2050 (Herd, 1999). Considerably sharper increases will take place in continental Europe. The process is already well advanced in Japan and will start evolving in most OECD countries by the end of the decade. In Ireland, the old age dependency ratio is forecast to more than double between 2000 and 2050. These changes will have important social and macro-economic implications.

In the medium term future (5-10 years), Ireland's demographic situation, in terms of average age and dependency ratios, is more favourable than our EU partners and other western countries. The increase in immigration in recent years will further improve this demographic situation, even if it raises other complex issues which are discussed below.

The challenge for policy makers in this environment is significant. The relatively favourable demographic situation should contribute to economic growth and a lower fiscal burden.

As the EU faces up to the policy challenges associated with its demographic characteristics, Ireland will need to define more clearly what its policy priorities are.

Beyond the medium term, demographic ageing has the capacity to change fundamentally both our society and the economic space in which Irish society operates in the industrialised world. Our ability as a society to handle the challenges posed by the phenomenon will be an important determinant of our position in the world economic order. How does the system deal with these long term issues and how does it articulate solutions or responses and build support for reforms, even though the effects are only likely to be seen one or two decades down the road? Our review of other countries indicates that this problem is being approached, in general, on a cross-cutting basis because of the need to integrate policy change across a large number of different government departments and agencies.

Immigration

Scale and international dimension of immigration issue

Running side by side with the issue of ageing populations and shortages in certain skilled work areas, governments in most developed countries and in EU member states, including Ireland, face a rapidly growing number of asylum seekers and illegal immigrants. Many countries with a shortage of workers in specific sectors have developed short-term immigration policies based on visas and work permits.

EU administrations are faced with the twin problems of (i) organising and co-ordinating a common policy on acceptance of immigrants and asylum seekers and (ii) developing procedures and administrative systems to handle the integration of immigrants of different race, colour and religion and culture to the host population.

Common European Asylum Policy – a key issue

Since the 1980s, the member states of the EU have been involved in the development of common measures in the field of asylum. The focus of the Council of Ministers in recent years has been the construction of a Common European Asylum Policy. This common policy – essentially a new regional refugee framework for the EU – will replace the various domestic legislative frameworks and procedures, which have been built up over the years in the European Union in the area of asylum and refugee protection.

It is intended that the cornerstone of EU policy will remain the right of third country nationals to seek asylum. As stated by Antonio Vitorino, the EU Commissioner responsible for Justice and Home Affairs, 'European countries have a long and proud history of offering refuge to those fleeing from persecution, war and conflict. The Union will continue, in conformity with the Geneva Convention, to uphold those traditions and to offer protection to all those who genuinely need it'. (Vitorino, 2002 P.5)

Cross-cutting measures required to deal with immigration

The implications of the immigration issue have a deep and pervasive impact on society and require a response from many departments of state. A considerable burden can fall on the host nation in the provision of health, housing, education and welfare supports for the asylum seeker and his or her family, and in facilitating their acceptance in society.

Fiscal Policy

The completion of Economic and Monetary Union (EMU) and the introduction of the euro with the associated fiscal disciplines set down in the EU's Growth and Stability Pact will henceforth be a key parameter of public policy. The rapid deterioration of the fiscal situation between 2001 and 2002 will also have significant implications for public policy and will put greater emphasis on the delivery of effective public services and value for money in public expenditure.

'In a world of increasing interdependence, fiscal autonomy of individual nations has been constrained. Ireland is no exception' (Honohan, 2001, p.1). Commentators typically distinguish between two rather different types of constraint; those that limit a government's flexibility in setting tax rates and those that limit a government's ability to run a temporary deficit.

Despite considerable recent focus on European Union commitments as a constraint on aggregate fiscal policy, these have so far been of much less importance than the EU's influence on tax rates and tax design. Market forces may however provide the most decisive of constraints and this influence is likely to continue to grow as far as tax rates are concerned.

If the external pressures inhibiting a completely free national decision on fiscal balance have been diminishing in recent years, the international influences on tax rates have been rapidly increasing. For Ireland, agreements at EU level have been a decisive constraint on indirect taxation. Apart from the complete harmonisation of customs duties, the replacement of turnover tax with VAT and the establishment in 1992 of minimum rates of excise, there is of course active discussion of common initiatives in energy and environmental taxes. Additionally despite the failure to harmonise corporation tax at the EU level, there has been continued pressure from some members towards reducing the distortions caused by differences in direct taxation as well as the complications caused by international flows of capital. Since 1997, 'harmonisation has largely been superseded as a catchword by harmful tax competition' (Honohan, 2001, p. 4) and avoidance of this within the EU was the focus of the tax package approved by Ecofin in late 1997 that has been in the process of implementation since then.

It is evident that, in a globalised world, differences in tax rates and tax bases between countries begin to be seen primarily as arbitrage opportunities. Naturally, the fiscal authorities of different countries are encouraged in these circumstances to start thinking about cooperative measures to eliminate such arbitrage opportunities, especially for mobile tax bases such as capital. The issue goes well beyond completion of the EU internal market and the OECD has become increasingly involved in applying this thinking to a wider international canvas.

What is seen therefore is an economic environment which demands a higher level of coherence from policymakers across departments. Industrial development, diplomatic and treasury functions require an increased degree of alignment in circumstances where external inter-governmental organisations draw up the fiscal rules of the game.

Conclusion

This chapter opened by noting the increased number of areas of public administration which have been dealt with in a cross-cutting way over the past ten to fifteen years. It then moved to identify the key factors which will define the political, economic and administrative challenges facing Ireland over the next five to ten years. These are based largely on analysis by OECD PUMA (2000).

In many respects, Ireland is at a crossroad politically, socially and economically. The enlargement of the EU will significantly change the political context within which the country operates. There is evidence to indicate that maintaining the country's relative competitive position will be difficult, in light of an increasing cost base, pressure for a greater focus on tackling inequality and deteriorating public finances. At the very least, it is safe to assert that the unique combination of circumstances which prevailed during the 1990s, including a favourable external economic environment and domestic stability and growth based on social partnership, will not recur to such a benign degree.

The changed circumstances which Ireland faces will pose very significant challenges for our public administration. Many of these challenges are more complex and inter-connected than was the case in the past and will require changed structures and processes to deal with them effectively.

Internationally, the process of globalisation and the explosion in information technology is increasing policy interdependence. The focus of concern for international policymakers is shifting away from conventional questions of co-ordination, towards the management of cross-cutting issues, which transcend existing policy and institutional boundaries. These global forces are producing cross-cutting issues which are not only numerous, but also have a fundamental impact on economic and societal performance.

3

Developing Policy on
Cross-Cutting Issues

Introduction

The review of global, economic and societal change in the previous chapter clearly sets out the major challenge posed in relation to policy development in Ireland going forward. Commentators such as the OECD (OECD, 1995) and NESC (NESC, 1999), have pointed to the need for new forms of governance to ensure that key institutional structures are capable of meeting the challenges and opportunities that Ireland will face over the coming years. In particular, the integration of planning and service provision is seen as a major concern.

So too, in discussions which we had with the Taoiseach, politicians, business representatives, trades unions, other bodies and senior civil servants, this point was echoed. Importantly, there was general recognition of the barriers which the current public service structures impose on policy development in relation to cross-cutting issues. Recent progress was acknowledged when the role of the cabinet committees and the Dail committees were referenced as useful forums for addressing these issues. However, those we interviewed commented on the fact that issues are now more complex than heretofore and are no longer easily dealt with by way of the traditional and legislative process. There was general agreement that new and flexible approaches were needed to ensure early identification of key policy areas emerging and the development of effective responses.

In this chapter, key elements of the policy-making process in Ireland for addressing cross-cutting issues are identified and discussed. We then reflect on our international experience. Finally, we identify the strategic issues for the future which are then taken forward to implementation in the final chapter.

Framework for identification and management of cross-cutting issues in the Irish civil service

Chapter 1 has dealt with the changes which have taken place in achieving the vision set out in *Delivering Better Government* of the effective management of cross-cutting issues. In order now to build on this progress, it is important to briefly review the context and framework for the identification and management of these issues in the Irish civil service at this point.

The overall policy-making model adopted by Ireland in recent years has been characterised by significant innovation and experimentation, on which the process of social partnership has had a considerable impact. At the heart of the process are the following key policy documents.

Programme for Government: In recent years, on acceding to power, new governments have brought forward Programmes for Government that set out the key strategic objectives for their term of office. The most recent Programme for Government has five chapters where the following five key strategic areas for action during the course of the current government's period of office are identified (Programme for Government, 2002): working for peace, sustaining a strong economy, ensuring balanced regional development, building a caring society and supporting civil life.

National Economic and Social Council Reports: The Council is representative of the social partners and adopts a problem-solving and consensus approach to the analysis of key issues facing Ireland, and in proposing solutions. Every three years, the Council prepares a strategy document for government which is then an important contribution to the partnership agreements negotiated between the social partners.

Partnership Agreements: since the first partnership programme (Programme for National Recovery, 1987), the social partnership agreements have been an important element in the national policy making and monitoring landscape. They have extended to embrace a wide range of social and economic policy issues and have formed an important context for policy making. In doing so, the nature of policy making has been changed, becoming more inclusive and reflective of varying constituencies than previously.

These strategic policy documents are complemented by an institutional framework of advisory groups including the National Economic and Social Forum, the National Competitiveness Council, and the National Statistics Board as well as other bodies including the Economic and Social Research Institute and the Central Bank.

Complementary structures have also been developed within government to underpin these matrix approaches including cabinet committees and cross-departmental teams.

Importantly also, has been the emergence of what Boyle (1999) describes as 'meta strategies' through a series of policy frameworks including the National Development Plan, the Health Strategy and the National Anti Poverty Strategy (NAPS).

However, as both Murray (2001) and PA Consulting (2002) observe, the SMI change agenda has tended to focus more on managerial issues and rather less than might be anticipated on issues of the quality of policy advice and support. As PA points out 'in general, we found the debate around policy formulation and strategy design is under developed'. They both argue that effective management of cross-cutting-issues is central to policy making going forward.

International experience in the management of cross-cutting issues.

In this section, the context in which policy is made in the countries we visited is sketched briefly, given its relevance to the conclusions drawn. Particularly illuminating from our study of international experience was that all of the governments under consideration had identified the need to deal effectively with cross-cutting issues as a major element of national capacity and capability. Whether the issues were largely of a policy or investment nature or of a service delivery variety, governments across the world are devoting significant resources to designing better and more effective approaches to issues which require mobilisation of resources across institutional boundaries.

What is striking also, particularly in the countries in Europe, is the degree to which social dialogue and consensus is an integral part of the policy-making process and is not called into question.

In all three European countries studied (Finland, Denmark, Netherlands), cultural factors and the education system have fostered a high degree of participative citizenship. Denmark is noted as having the highest score in an OECD 2000 review for fostering co-operation and working in groups through the education system. This pervades all interaction between the government and other agencies including the unions. In Denmark, one union official explained how the Danes felt that it was more constructive to be reasonable. He also emphasised something which was found elsewhere, the importance that the Danes, Dutch and Finns place on informal networks. These nationals will frequently try to broker a resolution to a problem through informal channels, with compromise as the preferred outcome.

Contrasting this with Australia/New Zealand is interesting. New Zealand has eschewed the model of consensus approaches for some time now. It is also difficult to point to effective formal models in Australia although a more inclusive approach to policy making and delivery is clearly in place as indicated through the *Australians Working Together Programme*. In New Zealand, having regard to the recently published report on the Review of the Centre (New Zealand Government, 2001), there appears to be a much greater preoccupation with stakeholder involvement and a wider strategic approach than heretofore. Indeed, it is evident that there is great concern about the lack of an inclusive approach and that efforts are now being made at political and other levels to address this gap. There was concern also about the need to ensure the quality and consistency of policy advice. Inevitably, this led to questions as to how to involve the widest range of people in the development of policy on issues which cross institutional boundaries.

Additionally, in both Australia and New Zealand, the focus is very much on performance outcomes and on straight-line accountability. The institutional changes put in place in recent years to support the focus on outputs and outcomes have been significant. However, the difficulties which this approach poses for effective mobilisation and co-ordination on key issues is now becoming apparent and was of major concern to the people to whom we talked, at all levels.

Against this background, key lessons are identified and conclusions drawn to assist in developing the strategic frameworks for cross-cutting issues in Ireland to effectively meet the challenge in the coming years. The key levers identified are focused on in the remainder of this chapter.

The role of political leadership in the effective management of cross-cutting issues

The various policy-making forums in Ireland, reviewed above, engage a broad spectrum of people and organisations in the business of government and provide a series of mechanisms through which complex and multi-level issues can be addressed. However, the role of political leadership remains critical. Strong political vision and leadership, accompanied by systems adaptation, is central to the new agenda going forward.

Three key areas have been identified as being essential to the development of the cross-cutting agenda from the political perspective (i) articulation of political vision and leadership, (ii) the role of the cabinet (iii) the role of the oireachtas

The articulation of political vision and leadership

The first major articulation of the need for the Irish government to take a cross-cutting approach to managing cross-cutting issues was with the publication of *Delivering Better Government* in 1996, which recommended that strategic result areas (SRAs) be developed for the Irish civil service in order to set out the key priority areas of government activity and the means of implementing them.

In his 1999 study on the management of cross-cutting issues, Boyle (Boyle, 1999b) deepens our understanding of a complex interaction when he points to a differentiation in the literature between strategy for the organisation, and meta-strategy, which is a statement of strategy for collaboration. In the context of managing national cross-cutting issues, the meta-strategy outlines the reasons why the collaboration exists and what it intends to do. It goes beyond the strategic objectives of the individual organisations, providing a context and framework within which particular cross-cutting issues are addressed.

Since publication of DBG in 1996, a number of meta-strategies have, in fact, emerged, most notably the National Anti-Poverty Strategy and the National Development Plan.

A clear legislative framework for addressing cross-cutting issues has also been set out in the Public Service Management Act, 1997 which sets out clearly the arrangements for the devolution of authority and accountability within the system.

However, a systematic approach whereby the political system can clearly articulate its priorities across the whole-of-government and mobilise a wide range of actors in support of implementation has not yet been developed.

At present, the major vehicle through which the planned implementation of policy is articulated is the statement of strategy, prepared by the officials of the department and agreed with the minister within six months of his/her appointment. However, as PA (PA, 2002) note in their report, there is a supposition in the process that the policies and outcomes have been clearly defined when the statement of strategy is being prepared. This is not always the case.

Furthermore, as Boyle and Fleming (2000) point out, while statements of strategy may make a 'nodding' recognition towards cross-cutting issues, to date there have been no formal mechanisms or procedures for addressing these issues either in statements of strategy or in business plans nor any mechanism for taking an 'overarching' evaluative approach across government either at political or administrative level.

Recent developments have recognised this reality and the new Guidelines for Ministers on Implementation of the

Public Service Management Act, 1997 and the Guidelines for Secretaries General and Heads of Office on the Preparation of Strategy Statements (Public Service Management Section, Department of the Taoiseach, 2002) which were approved by government recently, pay particular attention to the management of cross-cutting issues and provide a template across departments by which issues can be approached and by which evaluation can take place.

It will be particularly important to ensure that the key issues identified in the statement of strategy are in turn cascaded down into the divisional business plans and the individual performance management and development plans.

By way of illustration, examples of SRAs selected internationally are set out in the Box 1. These can provide guidance in developing future approaches in Ireland.

Box 1

Strategic Result Areas
Selected examples

Country level

New Zealand
Stronger families
Delivery of quality service

State level

Australian Capital Territories
Enhanced city planning, especially for residential amenity
Equity for indigenous people
Support and development for youth

Department level

Department of Family and Community Services (Facs), Commonwealth of Australia
Stronger communities.
Prevention through capacity building and early intervention.
Promotion of independence, choice and self-reliance.

The role of the cabinet

The doctrine of collective responsibility applies to the cabinet in its decision-making responsibilities. Thus ministers, in addition to their roles in respect of their individual departments, play a powerful role in policy making in their corporate capacity as members of the cabinet. The cabinet, as a central forum which includes all ministers, representing all departments of state, is the key central forum in which whole-of-government issues can be addressed.

For this reason, it is important to ensure that the issues which the government are asked to address take a whole-of-government perspective where necessary and that members of the cabinet have the quality policy advice and the time to consider these major issues. The processes by which issues get on the cabinet agenda are set out in Cabinet Handbook. Memorandums for government are to be circulated in advance by the department putting forward the proposals to other relevant departments for observations prior to their submitting them to cabinet. This process has become all the more critical in recent years as many of the proposals being put forward are cross-cutting in nature and thus overlap in the areas of responsibilities of other departments. However, there can be a tendency for departments to circulate memorandums at a late stage, or, occasionally, to bring their proposals to cabinet for consideration by way of an aide memoire without prior consultation.

As a result the cabinet agenda has become somewhat overcrowded and must be decluttered. In this situation, it is not always possible to identify the key issues and to accord appropriate priority to them. This is an issue which dates back even to the Report of the Public Services Organisation Review Group 1966–1969, better known as the Devlin Report (1969), where one of the major problems identified was the lack of time for the senior civil service to give thought to key economic and social issues.

Also, as we shall see in Chapter 4, the important process by which funding and budgetary allocations are made is generally conducted in parallel with the policy development process and by its nature focuses on the individual ministerial votes. Therefore, the procedures to allow the development and funding of policy from a cross-cutting perspective are absent and change is required if the Framework for Authority and Accountability under the Public Service Management Act (PSMA) is to become fully operational.

The Oireachtas

The Oireachtas has a central role in parliamentary oversight of the executive and in the development of policy and the passage of legislation.

There have been a number of innovations in recent times in the business of government and in the role of the Oireachtas, giving it a more powerful role to play. The implementation of SMI has brought greater transparency to the work of government departments and provides members of the Oireachtas with more structured mechanisms for scrutinising them. Statements of strategy, annual business plans and annual reports set out clearly the aims and areas of responsibility of departments and the results they have achieved in delivering on these. The Freedom of Information Act allows issues to be examined and reviewed at a detailed level. Oireachtas committees, established as part of the reform of the Oireachtas, are a vehicle through which members of the Oireachtas can hold the executive to account.

Recognising the central role of the Oireachtas in the system of government in Ireland, PA (PA, 2002) points out that the Oireachtas exercises the essential oversight function in relation to government. The report goes on, however, to comment as follows

> Routine parliamentary review of the estimates and appropriation accounts represents the key elements in the public expenditure cycle, and provides an indication of how much money is to be spent and on what services. Traditional accountability practices in this regard have evolved so as to provide an appropriate account of stewardship to parliament. To a certain extent such accountability can be ritualistic ... An ongoing

challenge for the Oireachtas will be to identify the information it requires to exercise its oversight functions, to articulate this information needed, and to ensure that the civil service provides it with that information in the format required, and in a timely fashion... (p. 104)

Boyle et al also comment on the issue of Oireachtas oversight from rather a different angle in their 2002 CPMR Discussion Paper *Promoting Longer-Term Policy Thinking* (Boyle et al, 2002). They outline the findings of interviews in which it was suggested that the focus of Oireachtas committee enquiries, as practised, is primarily on apportioning blame rather than on a dialogue on the longer-term implications of policy options and choices. In such a situation, it is the civil servant who acts cautiously who stays out of trouble, while those prepared to take justifiable risks and look longer term may face difficulties.

Although the Oireachtas committees have tended to focus on scrutinising the performance of officials, they are an important foundation in future relationships between the Oireachtas and the executive. The role enables them to address issues from the perspective of the whole-of-government that extends across the boundaries of departments and agencies. A future issue for government is to develop approaches which allow long-term policy issues to be addressed such that the Oireachtas can play a role in developing these issues and addressing any implications that arise.

The recent debate in relation to the EU is relevant in this context, in that the new procedures for parliamentary scrutiny of EU issues also provides a new opportunity to consider policy issues across a range of institutions. The most recent Oireachtas legislation in this area also puts in place a platform for a more integrated approach to scrutiny which can be built on.

Role of political leadership – international experience

In all the countries which we studied, political leadership was central to the role of government and there was recognition of the need for a shared political vision of what was to be achieved, underpinned by the action of the administrative system. It has to be acknowledged that while most countries have made progress in the areas of reforming government, none of them has been able to completely 'crack the nut' of developing policies and implementing them in relation to cross-cutting issues. However, useful pointers and lessons did emerge.

Australia and New Zealand each have a strong focus on a small but powerful number of key strategic issues. New Zealand has statements of intent, similar to our statements of strategy, which set out the programme which government will deliver on in the following years. In recent years, strategic policy documents have focused on clarity of goals and on outcomes achievement. New Zealand in particular is refocusing on this issue in its Review of the Centre programme (Review of the Centre, 2001).

In Denmark, horizontal co-ordination of policy formulation in different policy sectors primarily takes place through the party system in parliament, through permanent coordination committees among ministers, through permanent committees among top civil servants and through permanent and non-permanent committees at lower levels in central government. The budget procedure is seen as a major co-ordination tool.

Other countries appear to take a more active approach to the management of the cabinet agenda than has been usual in Ireland. They recognise the central role which cabinet plays in the teasing out of complex policy issues, in taking strategic decisions and in allocating resources. Some very interesting examples of management techniques, most notably in Australia, included:

- More active management of the cabinet agenda by decluttering the agenda of routine material by creating an A list for priority issues and a B list for more routine issues.
- Concentrating on a small number of key issues, often of a cross-cutting nature, through a series of planned presentations over a period.

- Putting in place institutional arrangements to promote the whole-of-government perspective by, for example, using a lead minister on priority issues.
- Developing a greater synergy between the political system and the administrative system through for example weekly meetings of all heads of departments, chaired by the cabinet secretary to discuss implementation of the agenda.
- In Australia, the Prime Minister writes charter letters to each newly appointed minister setting out his priorities and expectations of them in terms of policy delivery over the period of the government. The charter letter explicitly deals with cross-cutting issues and the Prime Minister has laid particular stress on the need for individual ministers to collaborate with colleagues on the whole-of-government agenda.

An examination of international approaches provided interesting comparisons with the role of the Oireachtas. In Finland there is a heavy emphasis on parliamentary committees and the leaders of the government parties will sit on these permanent committees in addition to whatever ad hoc ministerial committees they are involved in. The Prime Minister himself sits on key parliamentary committees, making him the key decision maker in the system. This is very time-consuming and there are concerns about ministerial overload. However, it is felt necessary, given the high degree of coalition government and the natural drive towards consensus that exists. The system is quite legalistic but very inclusive in that all legislation was considered prior to going to parliament.

In the Netherlands, working groups of civil servants present issues to cabinet and they are then forwarded on to parliament with the reaction of the cabinet. This is felt to be a very transparent approach.

Conclusions: political leadership

It is clear that strong political leadership is required to develop policies on a whole-of-government basis, meeting the needs of society over the longer term. To do this effectively, a shared vision of the type of society we wish to have in the future, and in particular the vision for the public sector, are fundamental requirements. Political leadership is central to the development of this vision and to achieving its objectives. This political leadership is currently articulated in a number of ways including in the Programme for Government, the agreement of ministers and secretaries general on statements of strategy, the bi-annual meetings between the Taoiseach and senior management of departments to discuss their business plans and through ongoing policy making and debate in the Oireachtas.

There must be a strategic approach to the design and allocation of portfolios to ministers and departments, that reflects the vision as set out in the Programme for Government. The allocation of clear responsibilities to cabinet, ministers, ministers of state and officials must underpin this. There is also a need to link the work plans of individual departments to the vision, particularly as they impact on the crucial cross-cutting issues, which currently tend to be dealt with at the margins. A single over-arching strategic statement is required, which would articulate the vision of the government and identify its key strategic result areas. Until then, departments will continue to develop their statements of strategy and business plans in isolation from the centre and from each other.

The role of the cabinet and the way in which business of cabinet is managed is centrally important in the effective management of cross-cutting issues. A structure should be put in place, chaired by the Secretary General of the Department of the Taoiseach in relation to the management of the cabinet agenda.

The role of the PSMA in this process needs to be reviewed and developed, as it is the primary mechanism by which the actions of the main actors in the system of government are connected. This needs to be mirrored in the statements of strategy where cross-cutting issues should be managed actively and down into business plans, PMDS etc. These synergies need to be explicitly recognised.

There is an urgent need to address the disconnect of

whole-of-government policy making from the budgetary process. Amendments to the present system to ensure a straight-line connection between policy decisions on cross-cutting issues and resource allocation are essential. This will be dealt with in more detail in the next chapter.

Greater clarity must be imported into the relationship between civil servants and the Oireachtas. The issue of how to make it less adversarial than at present must be addressed. There is a need for dialogue between politicians and civil servants so as to, as Boyle et al (2002) put it, 'encourage a culture where exploring options and trying various strategies is encouraged, in the knowledge that there will be some "wins" but some "failures" also' (p. 56).

The political/administrative interface

Ministers have both the political and legal responsibility for the performance of their departments under the Ministers and Secretaries Acts, 1924 to 1995, and the Public Service Management Act, 1997, as well as having a collective responsibility as ministers of the government. We review below the important relationships that ministers have within their departments which are central to the effective management of cross-cutting issues. These include the secretary general, departmental staff and political advisors.

Ministers and secretaries general

Ministers are responsible for policy formulation and achievement of the functions assigned to their departments. Secretaries general, along with the top management team at MAC (senior management group) level, play a vital role in advising ministers on policy formulation and development. They also have a responsibility for ensuring that policy is implemented and that the mechanisms are in place for delivering on policies. It iscritical that ministers and secretaries general have a close working relationship. These relationships have been shown to work best and to be most productive when they are based on trust and respect for their mutually complementary roles. They have been strengthened in recent times by innovations such as the Public Service Management Act, and the departmental statements of strategy which are prepared and submitted for approval to the minister by the secretary general. We have also, in some departments, witnessed the inception of the MiniMac when the minister and the top management group meet together regularly to discuss key policy issues.

Yet in the context of the relationship between ministers and departments, their ability to address issues that transcend the boundaries of their departments is limited by the structures that obtain and the 'silo based' nature of the system, including the limitations imposed by the budgetary system. The absence of institutional structures to facilitate discussion by secretaries general on the cross-cutting issues, such as we saw in other countries with weekly meetings on the cabinet agenda, has also militated against progress in this important area.

Ministers and officials

Departments are mainly confined to delivering on their own remit with little regard or perspective on the whole-of-government. In the circumstance where there is no clear prioritisation of the political agenda in relation to cross-cutting issues, it is difficult for departmental officials to prioritise these issues within their plans and there is no incentive for them to do so. PA (2002) concluded that SMI/DBG focused on public management reform rather than on a whole-of-government perspective. The emphasis on public management has overshadowed the other two elements key to the whole-of-government agenda – governance and policymaking (PA, p. 85).

For example, although the PSMA provides a legal framework for the assignment of responsibility in respect of cross-departmental issues, in practice the provisions have not been used.

Yet there are major benefits to be achieved in respect of better policy development from addressing issues on a cross-cutting basis. Significant benefits will also arise from the point of view of the system, as devolution of issues to appropriate levels leads to easing congestion at the centre and to issues being addressed more effectively.

Political advisors

The political advisor is a relatively new feature in the Irish system of public management. Their role, which grew in importance during coalition governments, has evolved to the extent that they have become part of the public service land-scape and a framework in relation to their role and function is set out in the PSMA. Much has been written in recent times about the role they play from the point of view of the insider (Finlay, 1998) and that of external commentators. As Collins and Cradden (1989) point out in their commentary on Irish politics, 'in particular, they help keep the Minister in touch with party political opinions, with other ministers and with outside interests' (p. 56).

The political advisor plays a key role in the management of the overall political/administrative agenda, in particular in relation to achieving a balance between the political imperatives as well as longer-term strategic concerns. This is well expressed in a paper given by the UK Cabinet Secretary, Sir Richard Wilson in March 2002 when he said 'I believe it is right that Ministers should be able to have special advisors to act as their political eyes and hears, help the Department understand the mind of the Minister, work alongside officials on the Minister's behalf and handle party-political aspects of government business. They can help protect the Civil Service against politicisation' (Wilson, 2002 p. 10).

Political/administrative interface: the international experience

Internationally there is a wide range of approaches to the management of the business of government and in particu-lar to the wide variety of relationships which exist between ministers and officials. These vary from extremely formalised relationships as in New Zealand under the Purchase Agreements through more informal and collaborative arrangements in Scandinavia.

The Australian Federal Government works in a complex environment where it deploys a range of approaches in dealing with the various levels of government with which it interacts. The cabinet secretary who is a political nominee, has access to both the political and administrative spheres, and is responsible for driving the government's corporate agenda forward. Government produces a series of strategic documents that set out its vision and work programme. Senior officials in the three central departments, i.e. Office of the Prime Minister and Cabinet, the Treasury, and Finance and Administration, work closely together to ensure coordination of the cabinet agenda and a co-ordinated approach to identifying issues and developing policy responses to government's agenda. Regular meetings of permanent secretaries, and meetings with other secretaries and state representatives, provide forums through which co-ordinated and collaborative approaches can be adopted.

The Netherlands adopts a number of structural responses to achieving co-ordination. It creates a new ministerial post or it creates a ministerial committee for a certain period. It will also divide up and attach pieces of an issue to each ministerial portfolio. Bilateral contacts, permanent committees and formal and informal networks are critical to achieving collaborative, cooperative responses. The role of the Senior Public Service, which aims to increase the mobility of the top three public service grades across ministries, is an important coordinating mechanism as is the creation from time to time of a single issue director general post to address certain cross-cutting issues.

The different approaches adopted in different countries provide models through which cross-cutting responses to government requirements can be made. The strong role played by local government in Denmark and Finland and the model of devolved delivery of services leaves more time for those at the centre to concentrate on the strategic policy issues. However, Denmark faced the difficulty of addressing cross-cutting issues in a whole-of-government way because of the number of bodies with which it had to interact and in response to this it is restructuring central government.

Conclusions: the political/administrative system interface

The relationship between ministers and secretaries general is central to ensuring that issues which transcend departmental boundaries are put on the political and administrative agenda and are acted upon.

At the political level, political advisors play an important role in the context of cross-cutting issues. There is a need for a forum through which ministers, secretaries general and political advisors can prioritise cross-cutting issues and can put in place the appropriate structures, resources and budgets to address these issues. The possibility of creating a more dynamic interaction between the political and administrative systems collectively must be explored.

At the administrative level, regular meetings of secretaries general and key officials in relation to the agenda should be established, specifically focusing on the challenges of managing key cross-cutting issues effectively. Although this is increasingly happening in the various cabinet committees, there would be significant benefits if the most senior civil servants met on a regular basis to discuss and find solutions to the most pressing whole-of-government issues.

An integral part of the response to managing the strategic result area approach is a review of the use and possible development of the Public Service Management Act, 1997 in relation to the management of cross-cutting issues.

The management of the administrative system in support of cross-cutting issues

Administrative leadership

The traditional structures, systems and working patterns of the civil service, established at a time when the business of government was much smaller and less complex, have remained largely unchanged and continue to be valid for much of its work. They are 'silo' based bureaucratic institutions supporting departments that have clearly defined remits and that address issues within their boundaries.

The need for different approaches to delivering public services has been recognised in the changes in recent years in the portfolios of departments and in some innovative approaches taken to addressing cross-cutting issues. There has been some collaboration by officials at senior levels across departments and agencies in addressing key strategic issues, including the use of cross-departmental teams, part-time teams, and collaborations with the social partners. What has been glaringly absent however, is the identification of one person in one of the departments/agencies involved, charged with overall responsibility for the delivery of the objectives of the particular cross-cutting issue. The omission of this critical element has meant that the tendency is for no-one involved to take responsibility. Furthermore, no-one is accountable for failure to meet the objectives.

The fundamental structures and budgetary processes necessary to address issues in a cross-cutting context are not yet in place. Such a move will be difficult to do system-atically because of complex environmental issues involved and differing cultures of the organisations across the public services. Secretaries general have traditionally operated within the bounds of their departments. In recent years, they have expanded their role to operate on a collaborative basis with their fellow secretaries general and various structures have been put in place to support this new role. The SMI Implementation Group is a focal point through which they can ensure that cross-cutting issues are on the political agenda and are prioritised on the public service agenda. By overseeing development of statements of strategy across the public service and by monitoring business plans and annual reports, they can play a vital role in ensuring that the political agenda is adequately reflected in the strategies and plans of government departments, particularly as they relate to cross-cutting issues.

The public service has been well served by its leaders

over the years. However, it is clear that new competencies will be required of the leaders for the future public service. These competencies need to be defined and put in place over the longer term. This need was recognised in a report from a group of senior civil servants in 2002 which brought forward proposals for the development of a Senior Executive Service to enable these competencies be developed and deployed within the public service (Aylward, S., et al, 2001). A government decision has now been made on this and arrangements for a Senior Executive Service are now in train in the Department of Finance.

The role of the centre

The successful development and implementation of cross-cutting issues is critically dependent on the role played by the centre. In the Irish context, the Department of the Taoiseach and the Department of Finance are regarded as having a central role in setting the context in which cross-cutting issues can be addressed. Both these organisations are seen as having responsibility for delivering on the modernisation programme of the civil service.

Boyle (1999) provides a useful template for the role of the centre in the management of cross-cutting issues. He suggests that the centre must establish the policy framework, engage in information gathering and analysis and monitor implementation and impact. It must use the strategic framework of SRAs to focus line departments' attention on the critical issues agreed. With regard to information gathering and analysis, effective information flows have to be established between the centre and line departments, across line departments and between the centre and the political level. With regard to monitoring implementation and impact, the centre has a key role to play in tracking developments on cross-cutting issues and keeping the main players informed on progress.

In summary, Boyle argues that a strong role for the centre of government is needed, when dealing with particularly complex cross-cutting issues. The centre must keep a focus on government priorities, establish the policy framework, engage in information gathering and analysis, and monitor implementation and impact. Murray (2001) also makes a number of pertinent comments on the role of the centre going forward. Referring in particular to the SMI he notes that:

> In Ireland, the guidance of SMI has been in the hands of the Departments of Finance and Taoiseach. This has paid off in terms of involvement of "the centre" and the incorporation of the contrasting mind-sets of the two, but it has also created a need for delicate balancing of perspective, power and pace between the two. It also leaves unresolved the locus of management of "whole-government" processes and issues. These latter, as noted from the very outset by SMI and DBG, are increasingly the pivotal policy issues facing society and government and it would appear that the matter is being sidestepped rather than confronted. A crisis of identity may lie in waiting in both traditional 'centre' Departments (p.9).

It is undoubtedly true that key players at the centre do not at present have an institutional forum for discussing issues of shared interest and concern – both SMI and wider policy issues. At times there is a lack of clarity of roles and responsibilities, which militates against the setting of a strong direction for the future. PA (2002) note that the role of the centre in ensuring a whole-of-government perspective on the modernisation programme and in providing appropriate institutional leadership will continue to be critical to the success of the project. The SMI Implementation Group can, in particular, play a key role in providing this institutional leadership. On the issues of policy themselves, PA state that they believe the Department of the Taoiseach should develop a thematic approach to the management of the change agenda (transport, health, social integration etc.) to ensure that cross-cutting themes reflect political priorities and that mechanisms are in place to deliver against targets identified in the statements of strategy.

The management of the administrative system: international experience

The effective management of cross-cutting issues is a central strategic issue with which all governments we studied were grappling. As already noted, no government has yet developed a solution to address this issue in a comprehensive way.

In these and other countries the approach adopted in responding to government requirements was that of 'agentising'. New Zealand, which had made most progress in the process, now has major problems in addressing cross-cutting issues effectively as the number of bodies involved in providing government services inhibits co-ordination.

In Finland a new approach is being adopted for the management of cross-cutting issues. The Prime Minister's office focuses on how to better co-ordinate the work of government and on strengthening coordination and co-operation in government. With other ministries it focuses on how to better define and co-ordinate planning responsibilities. Key areas being addressed are:

- strengthening the steering role of the ministries in their administrative fields
- strengthening citizen-government connections and quality in administration and
- information systems of government and the government as an employer.

In New Zealand the Prime Minister and her department play a key role in coordinating the business of government. There is a close collaboration between the Prime Minister's Office, the Treasury and the State Services Commission about the nature and direction of public management issues. The Department of the Prime Minister and Cabinet (DPMC) sets the strategic agenda in relation to cross-cutting issues and announces changes of goals when these arise. CEOs of the central departments meet on a weekly basis for strategically focused collegiate discussions. The DPMC meets with the CEOs for an hour each week to discuss cross-cutting issues. However, on an on-going basis each department makes policy for its own functions. New Zealand is also faced with the difficulties thrown up by the plethora of agencies which deliver its services.

In Australia, senior officials in the three central departments, i.e. Office of the Prime Minister and Cabinet, the Treasury, and Finance and Administration, work closely together to ensure close coordination of the cabinet agenda and a co-ordinated approach to identifying issues and in developing policy responses to government's agenda.

Conclusions: the management of the administrative system in support of cross-cutting issues

The existing structures and systems and the traditional working patterns of the civil service remain valid for much of its work. However, there is a need to move forward to respond to the demands that issues be addressed in an integrated whole-of-government way. Such a move will be difficult to do systematically because of complex environmental issues involved and the differing cultures of the organisations across the public service.

There is a significant role to be played by the SMI Implementation Group to ensure that the whole-of-government approach is adhered to. This would include the evaluation of departmental strategy statements to ensure progress on SRAs. They could also ensure that there are appropriate links between the political agenda and the strategies and plans of government departments. That group could also play a role in monitoring the annual reports to ensure they reflect the required progress on cross-cutting issues. The group could consider an integrated approach between statements of strategy and the allocation of resources through the budgetary process. The group could be chaired by the Department of the Taoiseach and serviced by a secretariat drawn from a range of departments and offices.

The role and structure of the leadership of the process at the centre, in Ireland jointly held by the Departments of the Taoiseach and Finance, must be consolidated, principally through the cabinet and the budgetary processes. Collaboration between these two departments must be maximised to ensure delivery on the cross-cutting issues agenda.

In accordance with the government decision, the proposed Senior Executive Service should be established and managed as recommended by the PA report.

Overall conclusions on policy development for cross-cutting issues

In this chapter the existing framework for the formulation of policy in Ireland has been reviewed. The roles of the various actors within that system have been examined. It is clear that cross-cutting issues must move from the periphery to the centre of the government agenda and be reflected fully in departmental strategy statements. However, for a whole-of-government approach to be achieved perhaps an 'overarching strategy statement' for government is required. There are already mechanisms within the system to oversee the formulation of policy. However these should be utilised fully.

For effective policy to be developed in relation to any cross-cutting issue there are a number of prerequisites.

At the political level, time must be devoted on a multi-annual basis to the selection of a number of strategic result areas from the Programme for Government. This exercise of prioritisation will require difficult choices to be made, but selectivity will allow policy formulation to be more focused, and implementation to be more effective.

For this approach to be successful, commitment to selected SRAs must be communicated from the top down. Visible commitment at ministerial and secretary general level will ensure that staff at all levels of the administrative system appreciate the importance of delivering on these objectives.

Leadership in various forms is thus critical – including the articulation of a shared political vision supporting a whole-of-government approach, and attribution to one person of lead responsibility for delivery.

Communications are key – good working relationships encouraged by formal and informal networks – all co-ordinated at the centre to ensure synergies are achieved.

Finally, policy, to have any impact, must be executed. It is clear that in tandem with policy formulation, the mechanisms for implementation should be under consideration early on in the process. This does not always happen. We turn to the issue of implementation in the next chapter.

4

Improving Capacity and Capability to Deliver on Cross-Cutting Issues

The best policy will be judged a failure if it
is ineptly implemented

(Scott 2001, p.35)

Implementation of cross-cutting policies

As identified in *Delivering Better Government* (DBG) (1996) and summarised in Chapter 1, the management and implementation of policies in relation to cross-cutting issues poses particular difficulties. These difficulties often result in cross-cutting issues being ignored, not addressed as priorities until too late or managed in an ineffective and occasionally chaotic manner. However, DBG's recommendations on human and financial resource management in the civil service did not include specific provision for cross-cutting issue management, for instance through teams and/or budgets.

As indicated earlier, the statutory underpinning for cross-cutting work was provided through the Public Service Management Act, 1997 (PSMA). It is interesting to note that in this respect Ireland is ahead of many other countries, for instance New Zealand, which is only in its second year of strategy-type statements and does not yet have statutory underpinning for cross-portfolio budget responsibility. The PSMA (section 12) also covers accountability frameworks for the implementation of cross-cutting policies. However, in general, budgets themselves are prepared and disbursed within the silo, even for successful cross-cutting programmes like the National Anti-Poverty Strategy.

At national sub-departmental level and at local level there are numerous examples of initiatives and structures designed to manage delivery of cross-cutting policies. Boyle (1999, p.1) comments that

> ...these initiatives have resulted in significant innovations, but one danger with them is that a plethora of initiatives can arise, each generating its own separate, independent structures at local and national level. At times, the range of groupings involved in issues can be unco-ordinated and confusing for the user.

This has been addressed in both *Better Local Government* (1996) and the *Task Force Report* (1998), which recommends an integrated framework at local level based on the city and county, and at sub-county level the use of area committees, based on one or more local electoral areas.

It is extremely important that Ireland enhance not just its policy-making capacity but also the capability of the administrative system to work effectively on cross-cutting issues. This would lead to very significant benefits in terms of the efficiency, effectiveness and value for money of the implementation of government programmes, the level and quality of service to the customer, the direct and indirect benefit to the customer and the organisational quality and capacity of the civil service itself.

In looking at the issues, with the benefit of our own experience in many different departmental and specialist areas, and in the light of our interviews with key players at home and on our visits abroad, we singled out as particularly important five factors:

- clarity and coherence of roles and objectives
- capacity to allocate financial resources and mobilise supporting facilities according to new priorities
- capacity to build the necessary delivery competencies, capabilities and skills and to adapt organisational culture to new needs
- capacity to adapt structures as necessary

- the need for accountability and evaluation methodologies.

In looking in turn at each of these five factors, the same
framework has been adopted as in Chapter 3. It includes a
brief overview of the principal features of each factor as it
currently exists in Ireland, key messages from the comparative
experience of the countries we visited and identification of
key areas for further debate and consideration and in some
cases practical recommendations.

Clarity of roles and objectives and the implementation of cross-cutting issues

Current position in Ireland

Over the past ten years there have been significant improvements in the clarity of roles and objectives overall in
departments and offices. The roles of the programmes for
government, social partnership programmes and statements
of strategy have been outlined earlier. While it is possible to
discern implicit broad overall whole-of-government objectives,
they are not part of an explicit shared common vision and
they are not used by the cabinet, ministers, the Department of
Finance or line departments to frame priorities in allocating
resources.

Comparable experience abroad

Implementation objectives were significantly clearer in many
of the countries we visited (these are discussed more fully in
Chapter 3 above). Strategic Result Areas (SRAs) clearly helped
focus on priority delivery issues and enhance co-ordination
of government activities. These SRAs are, generally, few in
number (e.g. nine in New Zealand) and very general in scope
(e.g. 'Improving the State of the Family') which find broad
consensus support. They are of considerable assistance to
line departments in setting their work in a firm context and
providing a mechanism to ensure that individual activities in
departments do contribute to achieving the overall priorities.

Conclusions: issues to improve clarity/coherence of roles and objectives

There are undoubtedly political and administrative risks in adopting a strict focus on a limited number of key objectives. In many ways it runs counter to Ireland's normal pattern of distribution of attention and resources – which tends to ensure that all issues and individuals receive at least some level of attention and service. Adoption of an agenda focused on priorities inevitably means that areas of lower priority receive less, or even no, attention. This is an area which requires significant further debate and is dealt with *passim* in the rest of this chapter.

However, from a logical standpoint, to achieve real progress on priorities, there should be a limited number of clear objectives which cascade from the overall whole-of-government programme down to each department's strategy statement, further down to divisional business plans and finally to the level of the individual as expressed currently under the PMDS system in role profile forms. Furthermore, it would be necessary to ensure that each department's activities in furtherance of the priority objectives should be the subject of discussion with other departments impacting on the same issue. 'Cross-departmental linkages are more necessary than ever from the level of strategic policy analyses through to the point of contact with the public (Scott, 2001, p.35).

The issue here goes beyond government making clear choices about strategic priorities. It is important that these priorities should be used to inform and set the context for each department's statement of strategy and below that again to divisional business plans of departments. This will facilitate departments working in an integrated way to achieve the desired strategic priorities.

Improving financial resource allocation for implementing cross-cutting issues

Current position in Ireland

Financial resources are currently allocated through the estimates process. This takes place in the context of macro-level decisions about revenue and expenditure levels – and of course within the constraints of the EU Growth and Stability Pact. It is based on each department discussing its needs and wants with the Department of Finance. While a multi-annual budget system (MABS) is theoretically in place for no-policy-change forecasts, essentially departments enter each negotiation round *de novo*. The approach taken tends to concentrate on allocations for the forthcoming year with little strategic focus. The availability of funding for new resources is further constrained by departmental reluctance to close down programmes which are ineffective or no longer relevant. The absence of programme exit mechanisms puts even greater pressure on resources, as new initiatives must be provided for alongside the continuing workload. This leads to structural and strategic confusion and severe pressure on manpower and budgets.

The focus on silo-based activities – which leads to and results from the current estimates process – is exacerbated by the role of secretaries general as accounting officers exclusively for their own departmental budgets. Given the adage 'what gets counted, counts', secretaries general will inevitably and logically focus on the best possible provision for programmes for which they are wholly responsible.

There has been a tendency to consider that activities without a specific programme budget are resource-free or costless. Two examples make the point clearer – the costs of serving the democratic process through parliamentary questions, representations etc., and the costs of the SMI itself in relation to the introduction of customer service, freedom of information, performance management and development etc. Both are apparently costless but in fact have significant direct salary costs, indirect costs from an increased corporate services burden and opportunity costs, because such activities require the investment of significant staff time at most or all levels both at inception and on an on-going basis.

Comparable experience abroad

Although the other countries we studied had all modernised their accounting processes – for instance, most had adopted or were adopting accrual accounting – no country claimed to have found the solution to the problem of developing exit strategies. It is extremely politically difficult for governments who must face the electorate to close down programmes, even in favour of improved provision. While New Zealand tried to provide for effectiveness indicators and stressed the pilot nature of new initiatives, they admitted that the difficulties remained virtually unabated.

Most countries visited also allocated financial resources by individual department, with their CEOs reporting on expenditure within the silo. However, they had moved significantly further along the continuum towards the provision of financial envelopes, with major devolution of day-to-day control subject to strong performance criteria.

After its recent *Review of the Centre* (2001), New Zealand is planning to experiment with new budgetary processes specifically for cross-cutting issues and to develop supporting legislation. These concentrate largely on an approach similar to our PSMA – as indeed does Singapore with its use of shared budgets with accountability by lead ministries.

In Singapore, New Zealand and Australia it was taken for granted that, when planning new policies where implementation of cross-cutting issues was being specifically allocated to teams, it was necessary to assess in the planning stage the financial requirements for essential support, e.g. specific accommodation (which can help to build a team ethos for longer-term teams), adequate office equipment and administrative support.

In the Netherlands, efforts were made within the budgetary framework to address the issue of funding for cross-cutting issues. Each department was allocated its budget in the usual way. However, funding for issues that crossed the remit of a number of departments was cross-referenced so that the total funding for a particular cross-cutting issue could be tracked. This has not had the desired effect to date, as evinced by the reactions post-11 September to terrorist threats, when adequate support resources were only given at the insistence of the senior civil servant responsible for coordinating the response

An exceptionally successful example of the efficacy of cross-development budgeting with even a small budget is the nation-wide juvenile crime prevention initiative programme that exists in Denmark called SSP (Schools Social Services and Police). The details are set out in the box that follows. It will also be referred to in the discussion later in this chapter on the adaptation of structures to accommodate cross-cutting issues.

Box 2

The SSP Programme (Schools, Social Services, Police) Denmark

This programme is a striking model of co-operation on a cross-cutting issue of major societal interest in Ireland. The programme, now established in Denmark some twenty-five years, provides for structured co-operation between schools, social services and police. It was initially developed by the Danish Crime Prevention Council that recognised that the penal system was not in itself a sufficient deterrent to the growth of violent crime. The programme looks at 'subjective prevention' which is aimed at making the individual choose actions that are not criminal or destructive. It also engages in rehabilitation work with children and their families where offences have occurred. The central objective of the programme is to build a local network that has a crime prevention effect on the daily lives of children and young people at risk. The law has been changed to facilitate exchange of information between the agencies in relation to specific individuals. The great benefit of the programme is that there is a very quick response from the system when a young person manifests a problem in any of the institutional systems concerned. Teachers, social workers and police derive major benefits from this form of co-operative working. The programme is undoubtedly helped by the strong civic-minded culture underlying Danish society, and by the apparent high level of co-operation of parents. The major lesson from this programme is that early intervention is critical. The three agencies involved in each area contribute to a central but small budget. The initiative also receives outside donations from the private sector.

A primary focus on expenditure control by Treasuries is a feature internationally and not just peculiar to this jurisdiction. However, a number of examples of flexible and strategic budgeting are evident in the countries studied. The willingness to devolve responsibility downwards and focus government departments almost exclusively on policy roles appears to be highly successful in the case of the northern countries visited, because of the centralised role of the implementing municipalities. It was less successful in New Zealand because of fragmentation.

Conclusions : issues in improving allocation of financial resources for implementing cross-cutting issues

Complex cross-cutting policies cannot be implemented adequately unless the necessary financial resources are in place on a secure but flexible footing. This requires full consideration to be given, at the earliest stages of policy development, to the level of resources required, the source of finance, when and where it will be spent, and appropriate mechanisms for accountability and monitoring. For cross-cutting issues this is more complex than for normal expenditure planning, which can be adequately done within a single silo. Where there is a lead department, it and the supporting departments must be quite clear as to the extent of their requisite individual financial commitments and how the lead department will leverage action. The costing aspects will be greatly assisted by the increased transparency deriving from the Management Information Framework (MIF), which will support the development of comprehensive costings and ensure that transaction costs (and equity costs) are fully captured. It will however require a high level of consultation and negotiation between the various organisations involved to ensure the necessary fit of planned activity and its associated expenditures.

It is also useful to consider the New Zealand example where departments can have more than one vote to reflect their several main activity streams. Where such a vote deals with a cross-cutting issue, it can be drawn down (subject to the lead minister) by other organisations. In an Irish context, this could be adapted to provide that each of the five or six main whole-of-government priorities has a separate vote. To protect this, it could be drawn up at central level at an early stage in the budgetary process. For example, where 'safer cities' was selected as an SRA, funds could be drawn down by a wide variety of actors ranging from the police and probation services to transport and housing.

'Seed money' has been successfully used on a number of occasions, for instance at a macro level through the European Structural Funds, and at a micro level in the Change Management Fund in support of the SMI. This could be further developed to support progress on the SRAs through underpinning priorities and leveraging real change.

As discussed earlier, the legislative underpinning exists in the PSMA 1997 for the allocation of financial resources for implementing cross-cutting activities, but this is rarely used. This should be much more frequently invoked where major programmes are involved. However, from the example of RAPID (where the excellent idea of front-loading expenditure in disadvantaged areas has been made less than effective by technical difficulties such as late agreement on budgets and the absence of any means other than persuasion to ensure compliance outside the direct hierarchy) and of REACH (where despite a substantial budget there is no mechanism for it to allocate resources to other departments for necessary sup-porting or associated actions), it is clear that the PSMA needs supplementing, e.g. by a shared vote specific to the issue.

Further development of the 'financial envelope' system (as already in place for administrative budgets) also needs consideration and debate. This was essentially a trade-off: greater managerial freedom for expenditure within overall budgets in return for more stringent reporting procedures. At ministry level in the countries visited, this meant that shifts of expenditure could be made on an administrative basis within a vote. This did not normally require parliamentary approval in advance, although there were robust mechanisms for end-of-year reporting by the accounting officer. This is not to suggest in any way that such movements should be effected outside parliamentary scrutiny, but simply that accounting officers operating within agreed government programmes and parameters should be trusted sufficiently to allow them to report on such movements at year end. This greater flexibility would help to ensure efficient and effective delivery, particularly on cross-cutting issues.

Overall, the budget process itself has the potential to go far beyond mere expenditure control to act as a strategic central unifying hook to achieve three purposes: ensuring that strategy is translated into delivery; prioritising resources – and if necessary cutting programmes of little or no value; and copper-fastening the link between individual programmes and the whole-of-government agenda.

The allocation of human resources to implement cross-cutting programmes

Current position in Ireland

As said earlier, the implementation of initiatives on cross-cutting issues requires first and foremost recognition of the need for appropriate resources to tackle such issues at every level. Dealing with cross-cutting issues can neither be a pious aspiration unsupported at budgetary and staffing levels, nor can it be carried out as an add-on to an already full job description. It is incontrovertible that not only must manpower be dedicated to the implementation of cross-cutting issues but also that manpower must be selected and developed for a proficiency in working outside silos. Elements of the Irish situation can be capitalised upon in facilitating work on cross-cutting issues. These include:

- a single unified civil service with a common grading system
- competency-based inter-departmental promotion systems which value teamwork
- internal promotion systems which are based on the same generic competencies
- informal networks which are strong because of Ireland's size and the proximity in Dublin of most departments.

However, those elements in the Irish situation with the potential of impeding co-operation on cross-cutting issues form a longer list.

- There is little real perception of the civil service as the common employer.
- Despite interdepartmental promotions, significant numbers have not had experience of more than one department, impeding mutual understanding and leading to different cultures and a silo mentality.
- Early experience at junior levels is generally within a single department, inculcating silo values.
- Recruitment is primarily directly from school or college, meaning that few civil servants have wide or high-level experience of the private sector.
- Congested, over-detailed workloads, especially at top management level, result in a focus on crisis-management and a shortage of time to invest in essential underpinning work on cross-cutting delivery (exit mechanisms are important here too).

Cultural issues

There is no additional credit given for work on (more complex) cross-cutting issues and the value of an individual's contribution to cross-cutting work can be virtually ignored by line managers. As stated earlier, such work can frequently be seen as an unwanted add-on and a distraction from the main focus on single-department agendas. Indeed, it may be more difficult to secure resources for cross-cutting programmes because of the lack of direct accountability.

Similarly, there are no financial rewards either for mobility within the civil service or for working on cross-cutting issues. It is worth noting however that some progress is possible in this area through the recently introduced programme of performance related pay for assistant secretaries and above and the forthcoming Senior Executive Service (Aylward et al, 2001/2). Given that civil servants at this level will almost certainly be working outside silos and across departments, performance objectives should include successful implementation of cross-cutting initiatives.

Comparable learning from abroad

There was strong evidence of the recognition by other governments of the importance of gearing the human resources structure, development systems and culture to foster effective responses to cross-cutting issues.

Structural issues

We noted incentives to move between departments (e.g. in Singapore and Denmark) which generated significant shared cultures and viewpoints. The Danish civil service introduced an initiative to encourage mobility between departments and greater networking. Staff receive a cash bonus if they serve in three different departments in their first ten years.

Where there was no single unified structure, as in New Zealand, state HR supports were put in place to promote shared values and ethos.

There was a strong tradition, particularly in New Zealand, of moving within the civil service and between the public and private sectors, particularly at senior levels. However, where open recruitment to top jobs was possible, it was found more successful when people with significant experience of the civil service were appointed. Netherlands was a case in point. It seems that there is a need for cultural understanding as well as generic management ability.

Cultural issues

Informal networks are more successful than formal. In most countries government departments tend to be located relatively close to each other, facilitating informal networks. Conversely, in Canberra we found that informal networks were impeded by the very scattered locations of government departments. One useful formal example was the senior civil service forum established in 1999 in Denmark. While intended to cover cross-cutting issues and promote better leadership, it had the benefit of encouraging better co-operation and networking between departments. A formal scheme of job mobility also existed – see Box 3.

Box: 3

Mobility of Senior Public Service – Netherlands

Prior to 1994 the Dutch civil service was not a unified employment and there was no interchange at the top levels between departments. In 1994 a parliamentary enquiry into subsidies in the construction sector revealed poor inter-departmental communication. There was a large debate about the advantage of management versus substance. Ministers were also reluctant to embrace change as they saw the civil servants as being very much their property. However, the reforms were eventually achieved. Interdepartmental transfer was made obligatory for all top staff (about 600) in 1998. It is expected to be widened to cover all civil servants soon. It is believed by outside observers that the scheme has tackled 'fossilisation' in certain key departments and that it has been successful.

As well as normal head of department appointments on 5/7 year contracts, short-term single issue director general posts have been created from time to time to respond to certain projects, e.g. the Milllenium Bug.

Informal networks were also facilitated by job mobility policies. In Australia, job mobility was seen as having an added benefit in that staff brought a broader perspective to programme improvements and ways to address any earlier mistakes.

Selection to work on cross-cutting issues was seen as a fillip to careers. For example selection was seen as conferring status in the Netherlands, and was regarded as a mark of achievement in New Zealand and Australia. A successful record of work on cross-cutting issues was recognised as important in career progression (and also as leading to useful contacts and experience in other departmental areas).

The separation of policy and delivery meant that agendas were significantly less congested, at senior levels especially, giving more space for strategic thinking generally and in particular for the in-depth consideration of cross-cutting programme needs (see below).

Conclusions : HR allocation and the implementation of cross-cutting issues

It is as vital to assess the human resource requirements at the policy development stage as it is to assess the financial requirements. This applies not just to a simple count of numbers and grades but also the development of the necessary competencies and capacities. From the Irish experience it is also clearly necessary at the inception of a cross-cutting programme to ensure that there is space and time for the identification of any cultural issues (particularly where staff are coming together from different organisations even within the civil service) and to build a shared vision and trust (Boyle, 1999b).

It is important to provide for a reasonable level of staff continuity, to ensure effective implementation of cross-cutting programmes. While this is an issue across the civil service, where frequent changes of staff mean high dependence on knowledge management systems, it is particularly important for cross-cutting programmes because of their inherent complexity.

There are also significant overall cultural aspects which must be developed to support a whole-of-government strategic agenda.

First, measures must be devised to overcome strong silo mentalities, both within and particularly between departments and offices. Some initiatives do exist to reduce this, including inter-departmental promotion competitions, shared training and development programmes organised by CMOD and, the most recent, the Senior Executive Service which addresses leadership development needs and the lack of mobility at the top levels. However, there are no overall planned mobility policies and many departments manage the timing of promotional vacancies to enable them to retain their own staff. It is extremely difficult for individuals to transfer between departments in the normal course. Induction training, where it exists, is usually carried out within the department. All of these contribute to the development and retention of strong silo mentalities. These mentalities impede collaborative working and the development of leadership capacities and they need to be overcome.

Secondly, different management and working skills are required for effective collaborative working – such as team-building, influencing, constructive engagement etc., and a different, more visionary, leadership approach. Any skills deficit in this area needs to be tackled.

Thirdly, it is necessary to find a way to give a measurable value to individual contributions to team or cross-cutting achievements. This requires attention to be given to aspects such as performance assessment and reward systems in these areas. To encourage optimum contribution to cross-cutting projects, it is vital that full recognition be given to cross-cutting project achievements, both for tangible rewards such as promotion (and merit schemes where these exist) and for the more intangible but nevertheless very real reward of enhanced reputation. Selection for work on such projects needs to be seen as a mark of success in itself and as recognition of future potential. Performance appraisal needs to take it explicitly into account (e.g. through giving adequate weight to the networking/team building competencies in PMDS). If performance pay is ever widely introduced in the Irish civil service, it would also be important that it should reflect the value of individual or team contributions to cross-cutting issues.

Capacity to adapt structures as necessary to implement cross-cutting issues

The Irish situation

The seventeen departments of state are all highly bureaucratic, with the majority as machine organisations. As such they have the strengths and weaknesses of such machine bureaucracies (Mintzberg, Quinn and Ghoshal, 1998). Their structure is centralised and hierarchic, exhibiting the classic traits of a control mentality, formal procedures, specialised work, and sharp divisions of labour. In today's complex rapidly changing environment, such bureaucracies find it hard to deal with issues of co-ordination and of adaptation and this impacts on their ability to address cross-cutting issues.

Network organisations have been seen (Snow, Miles and Coleman, 1992) as the way of the future. In Ireland there are some interesting experiments with stable network structures, such as the National Children's Office and the Food Safety Authority (see Box 4 below), which although small and flexible gain effective scale through their partnerships with other relevant bodies such as health boards. Their advantages centre on the ability to achieve excellence by focusing on developing and maintaining their own core strategic competencies and buying in other competencies through contracting out or partnership. There may however be challenges in quality control of the outsourced work and in resolving any conflicts which arise between organisations. Furthermore, where partnerships break down, the network organisation will not itself have the necessary capacity to maintain service and may have difficulty in securing the necessary expertise elsewhere.

Box 4

Network organisation: The Food Safety Authority of Ireland

There are fifty different agencies involved in aspects of food safety. Nearly 2,500 people work in these areas, in the past with limited or no communication even where different functions were within the same department. When the FSAI was established in 1998, it opted not to take over these functions but instead to operate through a series of networks. It reached service-level agreements with the various bodies, specifying the levels and standards of activity, subject to performance audit by the FSAI. It has enjoyed considerable success. However there are cultural challenges in working outside silos and in implementing performance audit and there are also pressures on budgets because food safety is not a core function of the other organisations.

Apart from the variety of institutional forms, in the Irish civil service there is also a varied level of recourse to the separation of 'steering' and 'rowing' (Osborne and Gaebler, 1992) by establishing separate agencies and semi-autonomous offices to carry out specific functions, often under a statutory mandate. This occurred most notably in the Department of Social and Family Affairs, an early mover in implementation of reform packages and now with a specific Social Welfare Services organisation to deliver individual services. It is also a feature of other departments such as Health and Children and Justice Equality and Law Reform. While it does in general promote efficient delivery, issues arise regarding lack of clarity of the relationship between the centre and the agency, diseconomies of small scale and fragmentation.

Some countries have found success through the devolution of implementation to local government or municipalities. In Ireland this rarely happens.

Achieving co-operation at local level takes several stages:

- formulation of a national policy within a sponsoring government department
- buy-in achieved from all other relevant government departments and from their agencies
- agreement obtained from all agencies at HQ level to free up or allocate staff at local level to deal with the issue, and finally
- complex monitoring and reporting relations put in place for all the different tiers.

These observations are interesting to note at a time when Ireland is giving considerable thought to local government renewal, (Better Local Government, 1996) and to the integration of local government with local development groups and initiatives (Task Force Report, 1998).

Comparable learning from abroad

In the countries we visited, there is significant evidence of devolution in different guises, e.g. the SSP as described earlier in Box 3. However, it was clear that devolution did not always work. Essentially the countries exhibited three kinds of devolution:

- devolution to a series of very focused agencies, as in New Zealand: this had improved financial performance but led to an untenably high degree of fragmentation and customer confusion
- devolution to a series of focused agencies, where fragmentation was addressed by the development of specific bodies to promote co-operation, as in Australia; this tended to work but at high cost
- devolution to centralised local delivery arms as in Denmark, Netherlands and Finland; in general this resulted in the successful delivery of integrated services with no customer confusion.

In the northern European countries we visited, governments have established a strict legislative and policy framework. They have made a heavy investment in the development of measures and performance indicators to monitor and ensure the delivery of the planned quantity and quality of services.

In effect, these governments are involved more in steering than rowing. Overall provision of services was highly efficient, although there could be tensions between different levels of service providers, e.g. in Denmark between the 14 counties and the municipalities. There are other debates: Finland and Denmark are anxious to rationalise the numbers of municipalities, as they are uneconomic when too small and there is a perennial debate about the value of the county layer in Denmark.

Although New Zealand had taken the principle of separation of policy and implementation very seriously, over the last years it has become clear that it has had major drawbacks (Review of the Centre, 2001). Policy making was taking place in an ivory tower environment and implementation was being hampered by a lack of strategic skills in the agencies. The service to the customer was less than perfect because of resultant difficulties in co-ordinating small single-focused agencies, often with different physical local boundaries. New Zealand has already started to reintegrate departments – for instance the Ministry for Health has now reabsorbed its agencies except for district level organisations. New Zealand is however very conscious of the need to proceed with caution in order to maintain stability and to avoid the high 'restructuring fatigue' which accompanied the reforms of the early 1990s.

The Australian government system is very entrepreneurial in nature. However, despite the real central authority of the Department of the Prime Minister and Cabinet, there were still big difficulties in co-ordination. In particular this could occur where the project managers were themselves from backgrounds resistant to co-ordination. In several instances specialist cross-cutting organisations had been established as an extra layer to ensure co-ordination between individual organisations. For instance the Office of Sydney Harbour Management worked with fourteen local authorities and the local infrastructural agencies to promote the harbour area, and the Office of Western Sydney was established to ensure a holistic programme to address disadvantage and poverty.

Regular meetings of departmental leaders is clearly important. In the Netherlands, the Council of Secretaries General – which meets fortnightly but does not generally deal with cross-cutting issues – provided the ideal forum to decide fast responses to time-bound problems such as the Millennium Bug and pervasive issues such as the 9/11 crisis.

Some views were expressed that structural reform, in itself, solves nothing – except to highlight that the government means to deal seriously with an issue. This argument says, with certain validity, that merging functions in a different way simply leads to a need for new cross-cutting approaches in other places; in other words there is no single panacea.

Conclusions/issues in relation to structural adaptation for cross-cutting issues

There is a view that overall government structures should move towards a network configuration and in the longer term technology developments may lead in this direction. However, for the majority of current government programmes, the existing bureaucratic structures have great strengths. Structural change is less important than overcoming the cultural barriers to operating across silos, whether such operations are between two or more departments, between departments and agencies, or even at times within single departments.

The evidence from the countries we visited shows that it is important to take a cautious overall approach to the establishment of agencies, especially where these would lead to a fragmentation of services. It is advisable therefore to take the following steps.

Make haste slowly particularly at central level – and adopt pragmatic rather than ideological solutions, which are easier to temper to the realities of the environment and the customer's needs.

Avoid over-concentration on setting up relatively small single-focus agencies or organisations which would fragment service delivery and confuse the customer, in addition to having high transaction costs.

Give consideration, in the event of a decision to devolve executive work, to measures to avoid fragmentation, such as delegation to larger multi-focus organisations like the municipalities in Denmark.

Building on the recommendations of DBG (1996) in relation to cross-cutting issues, there were a number of relatively simple steps which could be taken within existing structures to help implement cross-cutting programmes more effectively, rather than making major structural changes,

First, (as said earlier in Chapter 3) it would be extremely beneficial to have regular meetings for secretaries general to offer a forum for exchange of best practice, discussion of issues and difficulties, and the development of joint solutions in relation to policy development or implementation of cross-cutting issues.

Second, the Departments of the Taoiseach and of Finance, at the heart of government, must develop a synergistic strategic vision to promote a co-operative rather than competitive approach to issues. This is important both in policy development and in implementation. The two central departments should give leadership in cross-cutting projects and in strategic allocation of resources, and obviously can only do this if they themselves work together to ensure shared vision. This requires a closer relationship between the departments in people and policy terms.

Third, while working groups are effective tools, there are already too many of them and the issues they deal with are too fragmented. In the interests of more integrated government, and also in order to reduce congestion of the agenda for senior civil servants, it would be preferable to take a more strategic approach to the establishment of working groups. The costs of such over-focused groups tend significantly to outweigh the benefits. Those involved tended to meet over and over again with the same people, wearing different 'hats', and discussing broadly similar issues leading to similar conclusions. Instead, strategic overarching groups should be established to deal with the principal strategic issues. Individual detailed elements should be dealt with through a 'cascade' approach using carefully co-ordinated subgroups.

Accountability and evaluation for cross-cutting programmes

Evaluation is described by Butler (2002, p.9) as being 'at the heart of public service reforms' and as including three key roles:

- support for accountability, including measures to ensure that the programme has been carried out as agreed
- support for design and management of policies and programmes, through the life cycles
- support for learning for further action and development.

Accountability

In Ireland accountability in relation to inputs is strong. Financial resources are controlled in detail by the Department of Finance (with a 'financial envelope' system for administrative expenditure). That department also exercises strict control over the numbers and grades of staff for each organisation. This is set to change to a greater focus on outputs or outcomes with the implementation of the Management Information Framework.

One of the major obstacles to the process of addressing issues on a cross-department basis is that of accountability and its relationship with responsibility. This is a complex area which has been subject to great debate and consideration in recent years. At the heart of the answer to these questions are the twin foundations of public service values and clear and accountable relationships throughout the public service system. There have been major changes in these relationships over the last decade, including legislative change such as the PSMA and the Privilege and Compellability of Witnesses Act. There has also been a sea change in both society and the public service arising from various tribunals and from the Public Accounts Committee review of the Deposit Interest Retention Tax (DIRT). These changes are driving the need for the public service to implement a new accountability framework to enable it to address the issue in the context of a change environment.

In the majority of cases, effective accountability in all its incarnations lies firmly within a single silo. Where cross-cutting implementation is concerned, there are difficulties in assessing the relative roles, contributions and effectiveness of many departmental and semi-state bodies. Accountability is further undermined by the absence of firm interim and final targets, even for inputs let alone outputs or outcomes, and by a common failure to agree evaluation methodologies before the project actually commences. This has striking similarities with major ICT projects which come seriously unstuck because of factors such as the absence of interim milestones and of mechanisms to cut off failing programmes. Even where clear accountability structures are put in place, the location of real authority or responsibility may be confused. This can give rise to an almost perverse situation where a project leader is accountable without the power to ensure delivery. As Osborne and Gaebler have stated (1992):

> Except in dire fiscal crisis, most programs keep chugging along, year after year. Many politicians and

administrators have broken their picks trying to eliminate an obsolete program that still has a constituency. While the general public remains oblivious, the program's beneficiaries fight tooth and nail to protect it. The politicians win no friends but wind up with a determined group of enemies, who retaliate on election day. (p. 287)

Programme evaluation

The formal programme evaluation process, which is still in its infancy, has generally been conducted on a once-off retrospective basis in relation to single programmes rather than strategic issues. While it does provide a framework for evaluating policies on a cross-departmental basis, this has been infrequently used. This undermines its usefulness for whole-of-government planning. It rarely provides an adequate basis for the three key roles identified by Butler (2002) – regular measurement of achievement, contribution to improved programme design and management, and it does not leverage further expertise. It is clear that a new approach is required and that a major task has to be done in relation to addressing effectively the cross-cutting perspective and of 'joining up' expenditure programmes.

Scrutiny from such bodies as NESF and NESC has furthered progress towards enhanced performance measurement in Ireland. These bodies have started work on the role of benchmarking and the development of broad progress indicators. The partnership process has also contributed, through the Central Review Committee and other forums. There is also an increasing emphasis on regulatory review and an appreciation of the need to ensure a better regulatory environment.

Comparable learning from abroad

Formal accountability and evaluation was a significant factor in the Australian and New Zealand public services. Denmark has recently concluded a review of performance measurement. Most countries visited had moved significantly towards an output focus for resource allocation and accountability. This greatly facilitated the development of accountability, and left greater managerial freedom in relation to inputs.

The purchaser/provider split in New Zealand, despite its high transaction costs, has the benefit of fixing precise targets for each organisation and in making end of year performance crystal clear. In Australia, at ministerial level (through charter letters as described in Chapter 3) and at CEO level through performance agreements, the contribution expected of each organisation to overarching targets was also specified in detail. The strong role of the central departments in both countries also facilitated monitoring and evaluation – indeed the central departments could and did take back responsibility for particular cross-cutting projects, where line departments failed to meet targets. The Netherlands has performance indicators for outputs within ministries but as yet there are none in parliament.

There is a growing emphasis in the public sector reform movement focusing on outcome evaluation (i.e. a focus on the benefits to the community of the services or goods provided). Finland places strong emphasis on this. Australia is also moving strongly towards outcome measures as illustrated below in Box 5.

Box 5

Managing for Outcomes in Queensland

Community outcomes are agreed across government and provide the focus for collaborative, whole-of-government effort in developing strategies to achieve outcomes. They also provide the basis and direction for the identification of outputs. Queensland has identified eight community outcomes:

- a community of well skilled and knowledgeable people
- healthy active individuals and community
- a fair, socially cohesive and culturally vibrant society
- safe and secure communities
- a strong and diversified economy
- a good standard of living for all Queenslanders

- a clean, liveable and healthy environment
- maintenance of the natural resource basis.

Taking one outcome at random, 'a community of well skilled and knowledgeable people', the key outcome is the educational status of the community (proxy indicators being the % of students meeting national literacy and numeracy standards, % of students successfully completing Year 12 or equivalent, % of people aged 15 to 64 with post secondary qualifications, % of people aged 15 to 19 in full-time work/education or a mixture of both).

A cautious approach should however be taken towards the possibility of Ireland moving towards an outcome focus (for instance in the MIF). Efforts to go beyond output measures towards outcomes were proving universally difficult, although clearly beneficial in public relations terms. Outcome budgeting has undoubted problems in 'measurability, causality, control and time frames. The higher the level of outcome (such as morbidity rates, educational attainment, environmental quality), the less easy it is to attribute those outcomes to the action of a specific agency or department over a short period' (Simpkins, 1998, p.11). At a high level, the individual contributions of different agencies to high-level targets are virtually impossible to break down. Policy makers and service delivery organisations are currently engaging in the process of developing robust models but are finding the task very difficult. They find it therefore necessary to bring the specific evaluation indicators to a far lower level – and this comes perilously close to returning to output measurement. A further move to outcome targets in Ireland could however be kept under consideration in the light of developing international experience.

With regard to evaluation generally, there was a far greater level of academic debate and research on the public sector by universities and other centres of further study in Australia and New Zealand. The very real academic debate, particularly in Australia, stimulates, contributes to and in turn is fed by internal public service debate. Despite the efforts of the

Committee for Public Management Research, this academic debate is virtually non-existent in Ireland. Indeed, the Irish civil service as a whole has been described as deeply anti-intellectual, despite the undoubted intellectual capacities and achievements of individual civil servants.

Conclusions : accountability/evaluation for cross-cutting programmes.

The first considerable challenge is to make scrutiny take place on a whole-of-government basis. In particular, the move to a focus on outputs rather than inputs will be centrally important. A practical important immediate starting point is the development of the strategy statements by departments under the PSMA in line with strategic result areas and in collaboration with other relevant departments and agencies, where programmes have a cross-cutting dimension. This, in conjunction with the suggested vote arrangements for SRAs, would give an important platform to underpin scrutiny of cross-cutting policy development and implementation by the Oireachtas. The Comptroller and Auditor General would clearly have an important role both in direct evaluation and in his support to the Oireachtas.

There are two issues of major importance.

Clear accountability and measurable indicators should be put in place at the very start of a project. This means concentration on clarifying roles, allocating authority/ responsibility and setting interim and final objectives (or at least a mechanism for subsequently agreeing these). This is not a cost-free exercise – it will require significant investment of time. A move beyond output to outcome measurement may require the development or commissioning of supporting research tools, such as impact assessment. It is not clear that such a move overall has value at this stage in the reform and change process.

Building on these indicators, exit mechanisms should be developed for projects that have either completed their task successfully or clearly failed to meet their goals. These are absolutely vital to free up resources to ensure the achievement of priority strategic objectives. While there are undoubted political difficulties in terminating programmes, these would be eased by ensuring that objectives are clear and that evaluation indicators are set in advance. The objectives should be transparent and the indicators regularly reviewed in the light of their priority and effectiveness.

Overall conclusions on improving capacity and capability to deliver on cross-cutting policies

The management and implementation of policies and programmes dealing with complex cross-cutting issues in Ireland raise particular difficulties. Often, addressing them is treated almost as an afterthought to policy development. Improving this situation, which would bring significant benefits to government and the citizen alike, requires better focus on five factors.

A limited number of clear priority objectives – strategic result areas – should be adopted, which cascade downwards so that every individual programme can relate back to those priorities. The corollary, that programmes of lesser priority receive fewer or no resources, is difficult and needs significant further debate.

Financial resources should be properly assessed and allocated at policy-making stage. The budgetary process itself should move beyond mere expenditure control to become a central strategic tool.

The personnel, cultural and skills needs of cross-cutting programmes should also be identified at the policy-making stage. Cultural issues can significantly impede collaborative work: measures are needed to overcome strong silo mentalities. Mechanisms should be developed to reward, tangibly or intangibly, individual or team contributions to cross-cutting programmes.

While the current machine bureaucracy is competent for the major part of government, cross-cutting issues require a more collaborative overlay. Single-focus agencies can lead to high degrees of fragmentation and customer confusion. Instead, a number of relatively simple steps could effect practical improvements.

Clear accountability and evaluation methodologies for cross-cutting programmes need to be in place before implementation. These should include absolutely clear lines of authority and responsibility. Exit mechanisms for failed or outdated programmes are needed to facilitate prioritisation.

While these conclusions may seem simple, implementing the recommendations is not. They will require significant investment of time and effort, new approaches and new skills, and a renewed focus on collaboration and co-operation from the very top. There will be real benefits in terms of better government, better use of financial and human resources and better customer service.

5

E-government as a Cross-Cutting Issue

This chapter contains five parts; the first sets out the back-drop to the e-government issue; the second analyses the approach to delivering e-government in Ireland and the countries we visited. The third section takes a closer look at some of the challenging integration issues involved. The fourth draws particularly on the Canadian perspective on e-government, as that country has focused more than most on the longer-term implications for governance of this technology. The final section offers some conclusions on the cross-cutting nature of e-government.

Introduction

Is e-government really a cross-cutting issue in itself or, rather, a sophisticated tool associated with the delivery of complex cross-cutting agendas? Certainly, e-government seems different from other classic cross-cutting issues, as it does not generally involve competing or conflicting institutional agendas, at least in the establishment of its physical and operational infrastructure.

However, it is clear that no one government department, acting alone, can make e-government a success. Moreover, e-government goes well beyond the seemingly straight-forward rationale of requiring basic co-ordination of departmental effort. Administrations have discovered that even basic co-ordination of e-government services poses its own problems. At a more ambitious level, e-government offers possibilities for societal change that have far reaching, indeed revolutionary, consequences for the way in which government does business.

Genesis of e-government

The term 'e-government' focuses on the use of information and communications technologies by governments as applied to the full range of government functions. In particular, the networking potential offered by the Internet has the power to transform fundamentally the relationship between public bodies and the citizens they serve.

The origin of e-government can be traced back to the remarkable pace of development, over the last few decades, in the field of information and communications technologies (ICTs). By the mid-1990s, ICT had been used to engineer a major transformation of the private sector, reshaping markets and corporations. This was followed by predictions that the public sector would go through a similar transformation, with e-government leading to major efficiency gains. We referred in Chapter 1 to the new drive towards holistic government in the UK from the mid to late 1990s. In this context Perri 6 et al (1999, p.10) noted,

> ...the availability of advanced information technologies is one of the reasons why the prospects for holistic government are bright ... As the focus (of government) shifted to integration of services at the point of delivery, information systems have also moved to the frontline ...

How successful has e-government been in achieving this objective? Certainly, governments in all the countries we visited have been rapidly gearing up for e-government and many have committed to major ICT programmes, focused initially on simplifying and speeding up delivery of services to the citizen.

However, the very process of opening up new methods of service delivery has implications not just for service users and providers, but also for the broader process of public administration as a whole. The desire to deliver a range of services to the customer at one central point or portal inevitably leads to fundamental questions as to how the administrative system is configured to provide them. This point echoes the analysis of Porter (2001), Markus and Benjamin (1997) and Rockart, Earl and Ross (1996). E-government has, accordingly, become an important driver of reform in public administration with implications far beyond the mere delivery of services. It quickly embraces the whole policy issue relating to service provision and integration of government services. We include it in this review because we see it as fundamental to the future management of complex cross-cutting issues in the public service.

The current status of the Irish e-government programme

Ireland has been regarded as making steady progress on the e-government agenda. This agenda has been well articulated by the Information Commission (www.isc.ie) and the recent Government Action Plan, 'New Connections' (2002), sets out the strategy for the future. To help realise this agenda, the REACH agency was set up by the government in 1999 (www.reach.ie), as a cross-departmental team, under the aegis of the Minister for Social, Community and Family Affairs, to deliver integrated government services on-line.

The key task of REACH is to set up the Public Services Broker, which will provide citizens with a single system to access public services over the telephone, Internet or in person. All departments and agencies are required to co-operate with the REACH team and to make the necessary adjustments to their procedures and systems to facilitate the development of the e-broker. (Report of the Implementation Group for the Information Society Action Plan, 1999).

The central vision is to create a public services broker that will function as an electronic one-stop-shop where the public can avail of a wide range of state services. The target is that all public services will be available on-line by 2005. The Government Action Plan (March, 2002) notes some seventy e-government projects being progressed by departments and agencies and several departments now provide interactive services on-line. Ireland has signed up to the eEurope Action Plan 2002 and in November 2001 was ranked first for its delivery of on-line public services.

Examples of progress include: a centrally maintained on-line repository of information based on citizen life events which was launched in April 2001 by the OASIS project of the Comhairle Agency at www.oasis.gov.ie and a centrally maintained on-line repository of information based on business life events which was launched in May 2001 by the BASIS project of the Department of Enterprise Trade and Employment at www.basis.ie

Delivery slower than expected

Despite this promising start, the slower than anticipated speed of delivery in creating the broker is a cause of concern. A recent study by analysts Accenture, which placed Canada in the lead internationally for its transformation to e-government, placed Ireland well behind front-runners Canada, Singapore and the US (all 'innovative leaders') and countries such as Norway and Australia ('visionary followers'). While Canada has achieved about 50 per cent of what Accenture calls e-government 'on-line maturity', Ireland is just below 20 per cent, in a group called 'steady achievers' (Lillington, 2002).

In a recent progress review, O' Connor (2002) supports this view, finding that the country has a long way to go before the e-government project is completed. O'Connor suggests that a government chief information officer needs to be appointed, as no private sector organisation of the size of the civil service would decentralise IT to the extent practised in the public sector. Irish experts, interviewed for this project, who considered that serious challenges remain in the field of implementation, supported these views. These challenges arise, in particular, from a need to strengthen leadership and co-ordination. A source of concern is Ireland's ability to collaborate and integrate and to speedily embrace the structure and process reform that the e-government agenda entails.

Delineation of roles and relationship with the centre

REACH was intended originally to be an arms length cross-cutting initiative. Ultimately, however, governance became the acute issue, even to the point of it having an impact on operational and technical matters. Competing visions of what REACH should achieve, how and at what speed, ultimately forced REACH to revise its terms of reference. Governance issues have resulted in a move to have REACH established as an independent statutory body. To date this has not happened. It is worth posing the question as to whether it should happen.

Alternatively, on the supposition that REACH lacks power because of its situation within a line ministry, should it be relocated under the aegis of a central ministry such as Finance or the Taoiseach's Office? This would be consistent with experience abroad, given that in most of the countries surveyed it was either the Department of Finance or of the Prime Minister that played this role.

There are conflicting views as to whether REACH has been sufficiently resourced to carry out the tasks expected of it, and whether there is a sufficient understanding at central level of the complexity of the task which REACH has to do. The appointment in mid-2002 of a high level board, chaired by Dermot Quigley, ex-chairman of the Revenue Commissioners, is seen as a positive indication of a desire at the centre to give added impetus to the REACH initiative.

The role of the leader

The Government Action Plan launched in 2002 states (at paragraph 2.3) that '… a key priority … will be the issue of co-ordination across government to ensure overall consistency and coherence in the legal and regulatory environment'. Particularly noteworthy is the recent appointment of Mary Hanafin, T.D. as Minister of State responsible for overall co-ordination of the Information Society Agenda – a significant part of which is the e-government agenda. Given sufficient resources and a clear remit, this ministerial office has the opportunity to give the e-government agenda a higher profile in the political sphere and facilitate a debate on the whole-of-government issues to which this agenda ultimately gives rise.

In this context, an important question arises about the nature of the relationship between this new ministerial office and a number of agencies or groups dealing with e-government. These include: the REACH agency, the SMI Implementation Group, the group of assistant secretaries responsible for implementing the Information Society Action Plan, and the Inter-Departmental Legal Working Group which reports to the Cabinet Committee on the Information Society.

Structural weakness

An urgent task for Ireland at this stage is the need to co-ordinate agendas and bring harmony in interdepartmental developments. Despite interesting individual departmental successes by Revenue, Agriculture and Food, Social and Family Affairs, there are several indications that existing co-ordination mechanisms are not working well. An example is the unilateral decision of the Revenue Commissioners to move ahead to facilitate the filing of tax returns on-line, by contracting a private sector firm to supply electronic signatures to clients. However, dealing with the legal impli-cations of using electronic signatures and the authentication of documents is a pivotal cross-cutting e-government issue, and remains to be solved by the rest of the public service. Solutions to such fundamental cross-cutting issues need to be decided at higher levels of the administrative system, particularly if those solutions require legislative changes.

Questioning the original vision

An interesting question, as Ireland progresses towards e-government, is the extent to which, once part of the agenda has been achieved, this leads to reassessment of the original vision. For example, REACH has learned that the requirements of particular clients of the e-broker might be contained in a sub-set of the broker, accessed through special interest portals. They do not need access to all government departments and agencies. This may lead to a re-evaluation of earlier design and process decisions

A second interesting question is why some government departments are more successful at implementing certain e-government initiatives than others? Is it because for some departments provision of services via ICT is a well resourced, core part of their business? These departments appear to forge ahead. Arguments that this leads to fragmentation are countered by others who say that they cannot simply stand still and wait for the centre to arbitrate or for the rest of the system to catch up.

Thirdly, some of our interviewees strongly advocated mobility of personnel across departments as a stratagem to deal with e-government as a cross-cutting issue. As one interviewee said: 'when people know each other and each other's business needs, the chances of reaching consensus and rational solutions increase greatly'.

Finally, recent developments in the Irish structures for e-government demonstrate a growing awareness of the need for a ring-master at central government level. These developments represent an acknowledgement that a joined-up approach, working across traditional boundaries, is required. However, it appears that there is still a considerable way to go to bring the required clarity to the system.

The Danish experience

Denmark is regarded as one of the strongest performing nations internationally on e-government. In Denmark, the implementation of e-government has been identified as a cross-cutting issue that calls for collaboration at all levels of government. A government body, the Digital Taskforce, has the responsibility of realising Denmark's vision of becoming a world leader in information technology over the next three years. Denmark's main strengths are in delivering mature services in the revenue and postal sectors, a hallmark of the more developed e-government countries. However, the government's central portal is still organised around government agencies rather than citizens' needs.

Organisation of e-government in Denmark

The structures put in place to deliver e-government in Denmark were adopted precisely because it was recognised that the interests of stakeholders in the e-government agenda operate at very different administrative and political levels and must be managed in a new way, as a complex network of relationships.

The guiding idea is that primary responsibility for e-government implementation lies at the regional and local levels of government. However, it must be noted that, under the Danish system of government (like the Finnish one), the respective roles of national and regional government are very clearly delineated. This system makes analysis of 'who is rowing?' and 'who is steering?' much easier.

The role of the leader

The e-government project is led by a joint board, which includes permanent secretaries from various key ministries (Finance, IT, Interior, Health, Justice, Economy and Industry) and from organisations for local authorities. The permanent secretary of the Ministry of Finance is head of the board. Local authorities and local employers and employees are represented. The board is a structure designed for them – it is an initiative of and for them.

A second structural element was the creation of the Digital Task Force. This is located in the Ministry for Finance but its staff, 22-24 officials, come from eight ministries and local government organisations. Its purpose is to bring together elements of municipal, regional and national government in an unprecedented way, setting targets and co-ordinating initiatives related to e-government. It participates in planning, seeks to resolve conflicts between authorities and promotes the creation of joined-up services. Interestingly, this task force was expressly given power to resolve technical, administrative or legal 'show stopper issues' and to halt the inertia posed by them.

The task force does not provide subsidies. This was a conscious element at its creation. The Danes felt that if the task force were to have the power to give subsidies or financial assistance to bodies, this would turn the initiative into a centralised one, rather than one designed to promote optimum solutions and work practices throughout the system. The emphasis is on decentralising tasks as much as possible in accordance with Danish administrative principles.

A target of e-government in Denmark is that public sector functions should be carried out and services delivered in a manner that makes most sense even if this means fundamental re-organisation. They must be placed at the most logical, efficient and cost effective point.

While the Danish authorities have clearly gone some way to thinking their way through the organisational issues – and putting in place the cross-cutting structures they feel necessary to get the job done – in terms of e-government progress, the success of these arrangements has yet to be demonstrated. Nonetheless, the capacity and willingness of the Danes both to reflect on such structure and process issues and to attempt to design new structures and systems to meet them is striking.

The Finnish experience

Finland is regarded internationally as one of the leading countries for e-government development. However, unlike many of the other e-government leaders, Finland does not have a clearly articulated e-government strategy, or a co-ordinated leadership structure to drive the delivery of integrated government services. Although the Information Society Advisory Board is responsible for promoting e-government, ministries independently implement their own Information Society programmes. The Ministry of Finance co-ordinates information management and the use of ICT in government.

Until the latter part of the 1990s, the majority of Finland's work in bringing about e-government services had been about putting in place infrastructure to deliver it rather than making services available on-line. That focus changed in 1998 with government decisions aimed at encouraging information sharing by the use of development networks and spearheads projects. With its outstanding profile in mobile services and ICT research, it is clear that Finland is well positioned to benefit from the design of systems for accessing government and other public services through mobile devices. In particular, the seamless integration of mobile communications with the private sector on-line banking system in Finland offers opportunities for public sector 'piggy-backing' for payments systems.

The government has recently turned its attention to the issue of whole-of-government planning by creating a task force charged with the goal of delivering a government-wide action plan. Recommendations from the plan were delivered in early 2002 and address a wide variety of issues, ranging from service accessibility to co-ordination and governance structures. Moreover, it suggests that the Ministry of Finance, working jointly with the Information Society Advisory Board, should take a stronger steering and co-ordination role.

However, as yet, Finland does not have a single political or administrative 'champion' of the e-government agenda. Without that champion, it recognises that it is difficult to ensure collaboration or cross-working across each of the ministries to develop an e-government strategy.

The Netherlands experience

The Netherlands is ranked in the mid-range of e-government performers internationally. The Dutch government has adopted a pragmatic, consensus based approach to e-government rather than a clearly defined leadership structure.

Leadership

One minister of government, the Minister for Internal Affairs, is responsible for the e-government programme. Organisational change is a major part of the Dutch e-government agenda. This agenda involves research and emphasis on learning by doing.

The state agency ICTU is responsible for translating policy into concrete projects in the e-government area. It focuses on projects that are fundamental to the e-government effort. A key difficulty for the Netherlands is managing implementation across four layers of government – central government, the water boards, the provinces and municipalities.

ICTU is staffed by the public sector. It set out to have 25 per cent of public services available electronically by the end of 2002 (a goal achieved at the end of 2002). The longer-term target is to have 75 per cent of services (regarded as a technical maximum) available on-line by end-2006.

The Dutch e-government programme commenced in 1994 with a series of small projects. In 1998 the new government announced an initiative involving the creation of a portal site for some 1,600 public bodies and agencies. Over the past eight years, the emphasis has shifted from small scale, stand-alone projects to integrated policy making in which all e-government activities are fused in one new organisation.

Overall, the mood is changing in the Netherlands e-government programme from a free-for-all to co-operation. The ICTU's philosophy is that it is not interested in building consensus, as this will take too long. It tries initiatives and if they work, others will join in. Examples of such initiatives include the Departmental Intranet, and the Computer Emergency Response Team for Government Departments.

Incentives within the system to encourage integrated behaviour in e-government include subsidies and grants, benchmarking, prizes for special project development etc. At a political level, there has been a re-focussing of priorities from rolling out services on-line to using e-government as a means of securing back-office efficiency and streamlining.

The New Zealand experience

The State Services Commission (SSC) is in charge of e-government in New Zealand. Its aim is that the Internet will become the dominant, but not exclusive, channel of communication between government and citizen. The pace of change is varied. It is very active in education, and there is some progress in the health field. E-work opportunities are being studied.

The New Zealand government portal went live in July 2002. It is structured around citizens' needs rather than departmental silos or provider convenience. The SSC is convinced that the challenges of e-government will lead to organisational redesign. It considers that this will become obvious once citizens use the portal and can compare on-line systems with the pre-existing administrative ones. The SSC considers that, at that point, a debate will arise which will focus on people and culture, not technology.

The New Zealand government's portal will be the main front office. Big questions will arise about back office design. There will be a need to reassess skills. There will be changes to the kind of person to be recruited and assessment of how to retrain those who are currently in the system. New Zealanders recognise that an impact on organisational structure and process is likely. Interestingly, however, consideration of its extent and of how it will be addressed was not seen as taking place until after the government portal has commenced operation.

Echoing the experience of countries in the northern hemisphere, New Zealand interviewees acknowledged that generally, in relation to e-government, more clarity is required about the roles and responsibilities of the centre and of agencies. Long term the issues will be more about government and governance, than e-government *per se.*

The cross-cutting challenge involved in the delivery of e-government

Despite the public enthusiasm with which governments have embraced the e-government agenda, the achievement of this agenda is proving much more difficult and costly than first thought. Expected benefits have been slow to materialise. Our interviews with key figures both in the Irish public service and elsewhere gave testimony to this.

Few countries have examined the implications of e-government in a more systematic and comprehensive way than Canada. Drawing on both Canadian and international experience, Lenihan (2002) suggests that the prevailing vision of e-government has been influenced too much by early successes in on-line service delivery and misleading analogies with the private sector. Early expectations that e-government could offer a seamless service to the client may have been unrealistic. Furthermore, a failure to grasp the underlying challenges posed by e-government has left the policy makers ill equipped to hold an informed debate on the question. Lenihan also argues that in reality e-government may initiate the biggest transformation in governance since the democratic revolutions of the late eighteenth century.

In an attempt to explain these underlying challenges, Lenihan sets out a storyline to provide a broader vision of e-government. It starts fifteen years ago with the UK, Australia and New Zealand leading a government reform movement among OECD countries. These reforms drew a clear distinction between two basic tasks of government: policy and service delivery. The first cornerstone of the reform movement was that policy making was seen as a core function of government and, as such, was the preserve of government and public officials. In contrast, service delivery could be done in a variety of ways by the public or private sectors. As summed up by Osborne and Gaebler, government would do more steering and less rowing. A second cornerstone of the approach was the idea of client-centred service, which would make government user-friendlier by reorganising it around citizens. According to Lenihan (2002) this movement has heavily influenced the dominant vision of e-government in countries such as Canada.

In Canada, as in Ireland and the other countries we visited, governments jumped in to provide services on-line. Kiosks and websites represented an innovative way to deliver services. In most countries it is noteworthy that the services most frequently put on-line involve a simple transaction with a single department or agency (e.g. renewing a driver's licence or making a tax return). Electronic service delivery works well so long as the tasks involved can be defined clearly and separated easily. Such services are referred to as the 'low-hanging fruit' of e-government, easily reached by officials anxious to demonstrate the effectiveness of the technology.

What then of the expectations that e-government can provide a seamless service to the client? An answer to this question may be found in a probing examination of e-government undertaken by the Canadian government.

The Canadian experience: leading to a new type of government

A wide-ranging debate, about the nature of e-government, has taken place across the public and private sector and right across the Canadian federation. This debate (fostered by the *Crossing Boundaries Initiative* – detailed in Box 6 below) quickly acknowledged that even a simple interpretation of e-government as a way of making the delivery of government services more efficient by integrating or clustering them and making them available through a single point of access on the Internet has far reaching consequences for the organisation of the public service (Alock and Lenihan, 2001).

Lenihan (2002) considers the example of services for disabled persons. Hundreds of services for the disabled exist in Canada, which is probably the leading nation in the world in healthcare provision. Presumably, integrated service delivery should help disabled people by bringing relevant services together – to cluster them – around key needs of the client. But in reality what would seamless access to a range of these services involve? The example is given of a disabled person who wishes to apply for two separate services, an employment training programme and a transportation service sponsored by another department. What burden does integration place on the two departments to ensure that the services are streamlined and co-ordinated? Should the disabled person fill out one form or two? If the person expects to use the transportation service to attend the training programme, should that person expect the government to make them mesh? Should integration commit governments to aligning or harmonising programme objectives?

This simple example demonstrates that the very transparency offered to the public by easy access to e-information is likely to create an additional pressure on public services to integrate in a more rational way. Providing a seamless service will require much higher levels of co-ordination and co-operation between departments and agencies at both national and regional levels.

More importantly, the pursuit of seamless service delivery quickly pushes us away from the realm of rowing and back up to the steering or policy-making level. If governments really want to use ICT to provide better customer care, they must accept that seamless service provision implies a high level of coordination at the policy level and involves policy vision as much as service-delivery vision.

The Canadian analysis also recognises that integrated information provision involving the sharing of customer information across a number of government departments and agencies would require the creation of a single, government wide information system that criss-crosses internal departmental boundaries. Even this relatively straightforward initial task would ultimately lead to the need to create an information super-system, and an expectation by citizens for more streamlined service provision that would effectively transform the operation of government.

Box No. 6

Crossing Boundaries Initiative

The *Crossing Boundaries Initiative* commenced in 1997 in Canada. It is sponsored by more than a dozen federal government departments and private sector organisations. Its goal is shaping the direction of e-government in Canada. Since 1997, it has engaged hundreds of elected and public officials from all three levels of government, and members of the private sector.

In the Spring of 2000, four round table sessions were held in Ottawa, involving MPs, senior public servants, journalists, academics and representatives of public-interest organisations. Later, these were followed by a cross-country tour to provincial capitals where the paper's co-authors met with a similar range of people. In all, over 250 people participated. These discussions resulted in a paper which considers what e-government is, how it may change government and what must be done to ensure that e-government is not only faster, smarter government but also more open, accountable, transparent, fair, and respectful of individual privacy.

In the discussions it became clear that although e-government began as an initiative to improve service delivery, this improved delivery would involve a major re-organisation of internal governance arrangements.

Modern government is organised into a system of departments and agencies with well-defined boundaries. By contrast e-government operates through a system of informal networks. In Canada these networks are proliferating at an exponential rate. They are creating a new infrastructure that conforms less and less to existing government boundaries. So far, the old and the new have co-existed reasonably well, but Canada may be passing through a threshold where the government's centre of gravity is shifting from the old departmental model to a new networking one. Successful implementation of the e-government agenda in the long term requires answers to these questions. Only an integrated structure of management across government departments can design and implement this solution.

The Ottawa Roundtable concluded that getting to e-government would involve much more than creating a single window for service delivery. Integrating or clustering services requires a major rethinking of the organisational structure of government. This, in turn, requires strong political leadership from the centre. Ultimately, they concluded, the establishment of e-government in Canada should involve a Canada-wide initiative led by first ministers – the only ones with the authority and legitimacy to effect major restructuring of governance systems across departments or inter-governmental boundaries. This reflects our discussions earlier in this section on the role of the centre and the necessity for a ringmaster.

Following the publication of the results of the Round Table discussions, a national conference was held in March 2001 – 'Governing in the 21st Century' – its conclusion for government was that 'the challenges are rooted not in technology, but in policy issues of governance and leadership'. (Crossing Boundaries, March 2002)

Impact of e-government on the governance system (privacy and accountability)

The hierarchical machine bureaucracy, with its clear separation of functions, which exists at present in most western nations, is designed to ensure both personal privacy and public accountability. However, seamless government, which is the logical conclusion of e-government, cuts right across the boundaries that separate jobs and functions in the conventional machine model. In Canada, the emerging conclusion to this debate is that integration provides an infrastructure for a different kind of organisational model, one that more closely resembles a network than a machine. If this is so, fundamental questions exist for government about transition between the two models and the need for a strategy to manage the transition between them.

Implications for political leadership

Since e-government is about much more than the simple electronic supply of service, it raises, as has been demonstrated, fundamental questions about the nature of leadership, both at senior public service level and at political level. The move towards e-government will create a significantly greater public demand for integrated services. This in turn will pose profound questions about the organisation of departmental and agency responsibility. These will have to be addressed at the policy making level. A relevant question to ask is how many senior public service or political leaders are aware of the potential revolution in governance that may lie ahead.

Conclusions

What has been learned about current approaches to e-government?

Scale of the commitment

One of the most striking factors is the scale of the commitment internationally to embrace the e-government agenda.

Furthermore, in general governments are articulating key priorities for cross-agency e-government rather than leaving agencies to determine their own on-line presence.

Difficulties of integrating service provision

Despite the seduction of early successes within single department delivery systems, the more challenging aspects of e-government, which involve close collaboration across departments, remain to be tackled effectively. Evidence of this has been found in Ireland and elsewhere. Finland is struggling to come to terms with the need for integrative structures. Some aspects of the Finnish experience are also evident in Denmark and the Netherlands.

Inter-operability

The most easily understood problem for integration is inter-operability – that is, the technical differences that prevent departments co-operating with each other. It is relatively easy for countries to make strides to overcome this obstacle by setting universal standards and ensuring that procurement policy promotes the development of a single compatible system. Senior officials charged with the delivery of e-government confirm that the 'e' part is the easy part. It is in this area that the most notable success has been achieved to date. Yet, even here, the scale of the challenge should not be under-estimated, as indicated by the UK experience.

Slower than anticipated progress

In general, despite a reasonably healthy rate of progress internationally in developing e-government, there remains a significant gap between where countries are and where they wish to go. The technological ability of e-government has far outstripped its usability in terms of the present capacity of the political and administrative system to use it. According to McDonagh (2001), 'We need to make profound changes to the way Government works if we are to make the most of the new technologies'.

The experience of the UK, which is one of the most determined and progressive 'e' countries in Europe, indicates the extent that even technical challenges pose in achieving electronic service delivery. In September 2000, Prime Minister Tony Blair, when announcing a renewed drive towards electronic service provision, said:

> The scale and complexity of government, both central and local, means that the transformation required to capitalise on the potential of the new technology will not be easy to manage ... Government's track record of managing IT projects is not good, and the move to electronic service delivery will require very substantial work on the back-office IT systems. The changes required to the ways government works are likely to be an even greater challenge. (UK Cabinet Office, 2000)

This message was reiterated in October 2002 by the UK e-Envoy, Andrew Pinder, when he noted:

> Strategic planners within public sector organisations face complex decisions regarding the appropriate mix of channel deployment ... These difficulties are further compounded by the current lack of guidelines and mechanisms for public sector organisations to join up and co-ordinate their channel strategies. (Pinder, 2002)

Observations of best practice

Observations of approaches to delivering e-government in the countries we studied indicate that the most successful approaches are those that recognise the profound governance, organisational and integrative challenges it poses. These approaches include:

- *Strong leadership from ministers and senior civil servants*: examples are the UK E-Envoy, Canada's *Crossing Boundaries* Initiative.
- *Involvement of the centre to lead the drive*: this primarily involves Ministries of Finance and Prime

Ministers' Offices. Particularly strong in Denmark.

- *Common task forces and high level policy groups:* these groups should involve all the key players in regular, meaningful discussion to improve policy formulation and trouble shoot as barriers emerge. A good example is Denmark's Digital Task Force.
- *Adapting personnel policies:* civil servants should be equipped with the requisite skills and capacity, and incentives offered to personnel to engage in cross-cutting approaches.
- *Use budgets to promote cross-cutting work:* in the US all federal IT investments are scrutinised to ensure they maximise inter-operability and minimise redundancy. An e-government fund has been set up to support inter-agency projects to improve citizen access to federal services.

Relevance of e-government to other cross-cutting issues

It is noteworthy that recommendations deriving from these examples of best practice in implementing e-government are no different to those applying in managing other cross-cutting issues. Whereas this review of e-government commenced from the premise that this new, modern, high profile, cross-cutting issue might offer some new insights into best management of complex inter-departmental agendas, the conclusion is that the issues for management are the same. The results of this examination of e-government, as an example of a modern cross-cutting issue, serve to reinforce our general conclusions and recommendations on managing cross-cutting issues generally.

Key lessons arising from the study of e-government

The key lesson learned is that the real impact of e-government on the cross-cutting agenda of the public sector lies ahead. The powerful potential of e-government will create more pressure for an integrative approach. This will require fundamental re-thinking, re-engineering and the involvement of leaders at the highest level. The transparency – or window into the government system – that e-government provides will lead the customer to demand that the house inside that window be tidied up and re-organised in a more functional and effective way.

Despite substantial commitment of resources to this issue, governments – even the most advanced ones – are just at the beginning of the road in terms of integrated service delivery. The power of the technologies available to them is almost boundless. The challenge to administrative systems that attempt to avail of this technology is enormous. The consequences will be very far reaching and will bring about a revolution in the machine bureaucracy system which has served government for so long.

Ireland has articulated a clear vision of the e-future. The revolutionary consequences of delivering this vision can be detected in the remarks of the Taoiseach, Bertie Ahern T.D., in the foreword to *New Connections*, when he wrote:

> Information Society developments are transforming the way we interact and do business. This transformation is bringing about the single most dynamic shift in the public policy environment in the history of the state. The pace of change is without precedent ... the implications are generally accepted to be as far reaching as those of the Industrial Revolution. (New Connections, 2002)

It is clear that the transformational effects of e-government will be profound. With a few notable exceptions, this study has found little evidence that key political and public sector leaders have yet realised the extent of the transformation that lies ahead. It is a transformation that will test, as never before, the ability and capability of the public sector to work together in an integrated way.

6

Conclusions and Recommendations

In this report we have noted that over the past two decades governments across the world have engaged extensively in public service modernisation. We have made the point that, to a greater or lesser extent, they have put reform programmes in place to address two key imperatives – to make the public service more responsive to clients' needs and to facilitate growth and competitiveness of their economies. Despite these reforms, we saw how new problems are emerging internationally, particularly in relation to the management of complex cross-cutting issues.

We traced the history of public service modernisation in Ireland looking, in particular, at the efforts to improve the management of cross-cutting issues. We looked at the key drivers of renewal and reform which have accompanied Ireland's economic and social development. Drawing on the analysis of independent commentators and the PA Consulting Group's report on the evaluation of the SMI we assessed how Ireland has performed in relation to its modernisation agenda. We noted that substantial progress has been achieved and we reported the PA Group's overall finding that

> ... the civil service in 2002 is a more effective organisation than it was a decade ago. Much of this change can be attributed to SMI/DBG. However, the implementation of the modernisation programme is not yet complete. (PA, 2002, p.1)

We identified areas where progress had been somewhat disappointing. In particular, we singled out the management of cross-cutting issues as an area that was worthy of further analysis.

We found that the literature on public management had little to say about the management of cross-cutting issues. Equally, although the countries we visited offered us some useful insights, they, too, were searching for better ways of managing these matters. This led us to conclude that, in Ireland and internationally, this was an aspect of the reform agenda which was proving most difficult to resolve.

Why is the management of cross-cutting issues of critical importance? In our international benchmarking exercise we noted that the economic, technological and social environments in each of the countries studied are driving cross-cutting issues to the top of the public management agenda. These environments, because of the effects of globalisation, have now entered a state of constant change. Our principal conclusion is that good governance will depend critically on governments' ability to manage multiple vertical and horizontal layers of policy making and policy implementation. But clear gaps exist between the need for coherence and the capacity of most administrations to achieve it. Various changes in the way government is structured and work is organised will be necessary to meet this challenge. We found that none of the countries visited had developed complete solutions to these new challenges but that there are valuable lessons to be learned from their successes and failures to date.

This is not to say that Ireland does not already score well in managing its cross-cutting agenda. It does and we have noted several examples of good practice. But, from the standpoints of citizen/client responsiveness, economic and social progress, international competitiveness and an increasingly complex European Union agenda, the Irish public service is facing new challenges which raise fundamental questions about how it organises its work. We believe that the successful management of cross-cutting issues will be critical to Ireland's future success both economically and socially.

In Chapters 3 and 4 of this report we analysed in detail the key influences on the successful management of cross-cutting issues in Ireland. We looked at two aspects in particular, the formulation of policy and the implementation of policy in relation to matters which cut across more than one department's area of responsibility. We tested the current state of development in Ireland against what we found abroad and drew detailed conclusions, outlined in those chapters.

In Chapter 5 we discussed the cross-cutting implications of e-government programmes, internationally. We did this in order to illustrate how our conclusions might be applied to what is a new and very topical policy issue in Ireland and, secondly, because most of the countries we visited are grappling with this issue on a whole-of-government basis. We noted that while a state-of-the-art technological infrastructure is a prerequisite of any strategy, this alone is not sufficient to guarantee successful implementation. Rather, the market leaders in implementation will be those countries which successfully put cross-cutting arrangements in place to integrate delivery of the strategy across government and its agencies. We pointed out that the recommended approach applies equally to any of the more traditional cross-cutting issues, e.g. childcare, drugs, poverty etc.

In this chapter, we draw all of the above strands together. We outline our conclusions and recommendations and we identify a number of key areas for action. We do this to bring as much clarity as possible to our in-depth study of what is a complex issue. We acknowledge the progress which has already been made in Ireland but, equally, wish to emphasise that there is no easy route to the successful management of cross-cutting issues. Implementation of our recommendations will pose many challenges – indeed some will necessitate sustained effort over a long period. Some of our recommendations imply changes to the culture and ethos of the civil service. We recognise that change of this nature is not achieved overnight; rather it is more in the nature of a longer-term challenge for all of the component parts of our system of public administration.

Conclusions

We draw twelve separate conclusions in relation to the management of cross-cutting issues, together with seven prerequisites for effectiveness in this area. Before describing these we want to reiterate that most aspects of public administration are handled within well-established departmental and local structures. And for many of these issues the existing structures will continue to be entirely appropriate. However, there are an increasing number of issues which do not neatly fit within the existing governmental and departmental administrative structures. Our conclusions and recommendations address the management of these newly-emerging cross-cutting issues.

Cross-cutting issues are becoming a key part of public policy
Cross-cutting issues have emerged as a key element of good governance in the public service at the start of the twenty-first century as evidenced by research and activity on the ground in most OECD administrations. This emergence is driven by two key developments.

The first is the changing nature of the global economy and society. Problems and issues either emerge in a cross-departmental way or cannot be successfully managed other than through joint action across government departments and agencies. The second development is the way in which public administration developed in the late twentieth century where increased focus on cost efficiency has led to organisational specialisation and differentiation, separation of policy making from implementation and the creation of autonomous or semi-autonomous agencies for service delivery.

These developments have created a need for increased collaboration, co-ordination and a greater focus on integrated working. Responding to many of the most important chal-lenges of the twenty-first century (e.g. global environmental issues, the threat posed by international terrorism, ageing populations in developed industrial economies, immigration) will require increased focus on the management of cross-cutting issues across OECD administrations.

Governments have important choices to make in how they respond to the cross-cutting issues
Managing issues in a cross-cutting way imposes significant costs on administrations – a fact clearly recognised by those

administrations which have engaged most intensively in cross-cutting initiatives. Ultimately, the choice facing governments is to balance the management of issues through either single organisational structures or a more inter-institutional approach. In rather simplistic terms, the choice is between shorter-term efficiency considerations and longer-term or strategic whole-of-government effectiveness.

The management of cross-cutting issues therefore is a dynamic process. There is no right answer or off-the-shelf solution. Each of the countries we examined took a unique approach to the issue, although there were common elements to the strategies adopted at national level. Critically, international approaches to management of these issues are shifting and Ireland needs to have the ability to understand what is happening abroad and adapt best practice to domestic conditions. Despite the success of the last decade, Ireland has to improve the way it manages these issues.

Ireland has done some good work in its approach to cross-cutting issues in recent years

It is clear that key areas of the Irish public service recognise the need for effective cross-cutting strategies. We have cited examples in the text where successful initiatives have realised tangible results and we have explained the factors behind these successes. At a macro-economic level some of the key successes of the past decade have been driven by concepts and institutions which, if not explicitly cross-cutting in nature, have certainly worked in this way – social partnership being the primary example.

However, there is more work to do. On the economic side, the principal challenge for Ireland is to make the step change from competitiveness as a location for capital investment to competitiveness based on a higher value-added model in a changed climate of international economic decision making. This challenge is based, at least in part, on the evolution of knowledge-based societies in the leading industrialised economies.

Ultimately, this requires that important elements of the economic strategy that has brought the Irish economy to its current point must now be challenged and, if necessary, dispensed with and replaced with more appropriate strategies. The scope and nature of this challenge means it can only be approached on a cross-cutting basis. An example of this challenge would arise in the area of physical infrastructure, in particular in the communications and energy sectors that are subject to liberalisation and internationalisation. The role of the civil service extends from dealing with the adequacy of basic infrastructure to the need to create regulatory environments which support higher levels of infrastructure investment by the private sector. Regional and social policy objectives aimed at ensuring access to that infrastructure across all segments of society and all areas of the economy are also *ad rem*.

Effective management of cross-cutting issues requires countries to adopt solutions which reflect domestic priorities

Four of the key lessons from our analysis of international approaches to cross-cutting issues are particularly important to highlight as conclusions.

The first conclusion is fairly obvious – national approaches to management of cross-cutting issues depend critically on each country's point of departure – in other words – what you do really depends on where you are. The point of departure varies substantially across countries in terms of both the distribution of functions across government departments and agencies and the distribution of discretionary power across those departments and agencies. The range of approaches adopted in the different countries we have analysed reflects the variety in these two fundamental parameters of government.

The second conclusion here is that, while effective cross-cutting approaches are necessary and are applied in the case of both short term crises and longer term management, those countries which manage cross-cutting space most effectively appear to engage in these approaches primarily with a view to addressing longer term issues.

Furthermore, the longer-term strategic emphasis extends to management of public policy generally in these countries

– in other words it is not applied solely in the area of cross-cutting management. The approach to cross-cutting issues is also culture bound and is supported by explicit and implicit cultural values in the administrative system. More generally, we have found that it is not possible to develop and sustain values in the cross-cutting space that do not find expression and support in the individual institutions from which the resources drawn for cross-cutting efforts are sourced. In each country's cross-cutting structures and processes, we have found a cross-section of the values that underpin the operation of the system of public administration generally in that economy.

Finally, there appears to be a clear relationship between effective long-term management of the cross-cutting space and effective short-term deployment of resources and structures. In other words, the notion that cross-cutting management automatically leads to higher overall costs of public administration is not universally supported by the evidence found in the public administrations examined. Essentially, the longer-term benefits of working in this way can out-weigh the associated costs.

The 'agency' culture can seriously damage the capacity of government to act as a unit

In addition to examining the strengths of other countries' approaches to managing the cross-cutting space, we have been able to see some of the developments internationally which may have impeded or offset progress made in understanding cross-cutting issues.

A good example is New Zealand, which, having gone very far down the agentisation track, is now attempting to retrench. Equally, although we were impressed by the many benefits arising from decentralised local government in Scandinavia, we also became aware of the difficulties posed for efficient delivery of public services due to the size of many of the local authorities delivering a wide range of public services. Here, we concluded that, even where administrations tackle cross-cutting issues relatively effectively, the need to operate efficiently within institutional structures can re-assert itself.

Nothing is more important than culture in managing cross-cutting issues effectively

Organisational culture and sound structural configuration are most important in relation to the longer-term capacity to manage these issues.

The machine bureaucracy model still remains the basic structural component of the public administration system despite all its potential weaknesses. However, the machine bureaucracy, geared towards silo-based objectives and culture, is not well adapted for horizontal co-ordination and will experience real problems in coping with cross-cutting agendas.

We have seen the advantages when somewhat different cultural values underpin the system of public administration, and there is structural configuration in which central government does not find itself engaged in and responsible for the full gamut of public administration. In those circumstances, a capability within the administrative system to adapt structure provides the critical pre-conditions for structural change to happen in response to emerging problems of a cross-cutting nature.

Approaches to managing cross-cutting issues can be tackled as part of the SMI

Important aspects of the Strategic Management Initiative are still being bedded down in the Irish public service. There is a clear view that eight years is not very long in the scheme of managing fundamental change and reform of the Irish public service. There is still scope for the SMI to consolidate further and yield results and the recent external review highlights what still needs to be done.

Our view, however, is not just that the SMI still has a lot to offer, but that the process of reform should be accelerated in a number of key areas. This is necessary if the public service is to be in a position to meet the challenges of the next decade – some of the most important aspects of the further steps required relate to the capacity of the system to handle cross-cutting issues. We deal with a number of the key changes required in the reform programme in our recommendations.

Cross-cutting = policy + implementation.

As is clear from the previous section, cross-cutting actions are at least as much about 'doing' as they are about 'thinking'. We see a danger of the Irish public administration system thinking itself to optimal solutions in cross-cutting issues before it even begins to consider the essentials of how best to actually deliver on the cross-cutting agenda.

Clearly, judging from our analysis of international experience, it is not enough to decide at the policy level what issues are important. Unless that policy decision is supported by the right implementation procedures, the initiative will be doomed to failure. A policy without implementation is worse than having no policy at all because non-implemented policy is a classic tool under which institutional interest can block unwanted cross-cutting initiatives. We cannot over-emphasise the importance of implementation strategies and this is why we have devoted an entire chapter to these issues.

Budget frameworks can impact significantly on cross-cutting effectiveness.

A fresh approach to budgeting is imperative if cross-cutting issues are to be properly resourced and realised. The position at present is that budgets are not allocated for the management of a particular cross-cutting project. The handling of a cross-cutting project is frequently seen as an add-on to an individual's job and a department's work. The allocation of resources, specifically for cross-cutting issues, would not only contribute to their successful outcome but would enhance their importance within the participating departments. We have seen abroad that even the allocation of very small budgets for a specific cross-cutting outcome can have significant benefits.

Leadership matters too!

Although cross-cutting issues will involve more than one department, they must ultimately fall under one lead person/department's responsibility. It is also imperative that the accountability aspect is addressed. Experience shows that where no single department or individual has a lead role/responsibility, projects can fall between stools. International experience has shown that where one senior person, either at ministerial or secretary general level, is given responsibility for a cross-cutting issue/group of cross-cutting issues (even on a stand alone basis), the results are very good.

An effective exit strategy would assist in creating the space required for cross-cutting action

Many political and public administration systems internationally suffer from an inability to drop programmes which are ineffective, underachieving or just no longer required. This can result in overload at the centre of government and reduces administrative capacity generally, particularly for those cross-cutting actions which may sit at the periphery of institutional agendas. There is a clear need for strategies to review the ongoing viability of programmes and, where appropriate, to cut expenditure and drop programmes. Such an approach would assist in the quality of public administration generally and especially with regard to cross-cutting actions.

It is clear that Ireland lacks exit strategies to assess programmes that are not working and to make the decision to terminate them. This tendency has been compounded by the rate of economic growth in recent years and, in particular, by the rate of increase in public expenditure in the more recent past. The tendency generally is, once a programme is established, to cut it for budgetary reasons only. If we are to be serious about cross-cutting issues, we must be prepared to evaluate expenditure and cull out-moded departmental programmes more effectively.

Cross-cutting issues present an exciting challenge to senior public servants

Contrary to what one might expect, it seems that monetary rewards are not essential to the motivation of staff involved in cross-cutting issues. International experience suggests that where cross-cutting issues are given importance, staff see their assignment to the management of such issues as conferring status. They further see them as helping them in future career advancement. We have seen many examples of how the development of staff and their increased mobility around the public service can contribute both to personal job satisfaction and the optimum use of talent on behalf of the government. It is encouraging to conclude that the public service constraints on monetary reward are not necessarily a limitation.

Seven absolute pre-requisites to effective management of cross-cutting issues

Based on our analysis of approaches to management of cross-cutting issues in the countries visited, we have identified seven key pre-requisites to effectiveness in this area.

Analyse and choose between competing issues: because at the core of the management of cross-cutting issues is the capacity to determine where to focus resources and where not to focus resources. This arises because the universe of potential cross-cutting issues is always greater than the capacity of the system to manage them effectively.

Concentrate resources on effective execution: because a system without deployment capacity will invariably fail to optimise cross-cutting management. Included in this concept is the capacity to analyse effectively what is going on in the cross-cutting space. Two key issues are the importance of deploying the right structures and the allocation of responsibility for implementation at every level within the system. Good results invariably require good diagnostic systems.

Involve both the political and administrative systems: the effective management of cross-cutting issues stems from a shared agenda at political and administrative levels and systems to facilitate ongoing dialogue between both.

Enable the political system to lead and support cross-cutting processes: political leadership and support are necessary parts of the whole-of-government approach and have a crucial role to play in specifying departmental objectives, resource base and values required in effective cross-cutting action.

Adapt institutional structures and processes: the old maxim 'structure before strategy' applies also to the management of cross-cutting issues. The traditional departmental structure has stood the test of time but it does have its limitations. Cross-cutting issues demand new approaches to structures and processes – in particular, a greater emphasis on team-based working.

Adapt behaviour across departments and agencies: silo-driven mentalities are an obstacle to cross-cutting initiatives. They result in institutional conflict or power-based negotiation rather than clear-headed focus on open-minded approaches to issue resolution. EU enlargement, for example, poses particular challenges and underlines the need for successful coalition building across a wide variety of interests, in order to achieve national objectives.

Develop robust evaluation systems: because without evaluation, mistakes will be repeated and good practice will not be captured for the future and the opportunity to refine the management of cross-cutting issues will be lost.

The pre-requisites listed above produce the linkages between political philosophy, administrative values, strategic agenda and institutional capacity necessary for effective cross-cutting management across the public service.

Recommendations : Context

Our recommendations are designed with three objectives in mind: to broaden the frame of reference of policy makers to encompass cross-cutting issues; to strengthen the incentives for cross-cutting working; to improve the capacity of the system to implement cross-cutting policies by focusing on resources, structures, skills, objective-setting and evaluation methodologies.

Our recommendations build on those contained in *Delivering Better Government* and other recent reports on the management of cross-cutting issues internationally. More particularly, our recommendations address the question of how to give effect to the seven pre-requisites to effective management of cross-cutting issues which we have already outlined.

Implementation of the recommendations will not impose any significant additional costs on the Exchequer. They will, however, require a basic shift in how work is organised. In essence, they call for fundamental changes in communications structures within and between the political and administrative systems. This will entail top-down and bottom-up approaches to formulation of policy and its implementation in a cross-cutting context. Our recommendations also call for a more disciplined approach to prioritising issues of national importance.

We have approached the management of cross-cutting issues from two aspects, policy formulation and policy implementation. Equally, there are two recurring themes running through our recommendations. One is the role which the various stakeholders in our political and administrative systems must play in the successful management of the cross-cutting agenda. The second is the implementation strategies which must be put in place to deliver on this agenda. Before outlining our recommendations, we first develop these two themes in some detail.

Stakeholders' roles

Our recommendations are addressed to the various stakeholders who have a key role to play in the effective management of cross-cutting issues. The effective management of cross-cutting issues requires a whole-of-government approach. We therefore cover the role of political leadership, the role of the cabinet, the role of the Oireachtas, the role of ministers in the development of policy and the role of civil servants in advising on and implementation of these policies. Most importantly, our recommendations emphasise the need for a proper 'connect' between these three distinct areas of the whole-of-government approach.

We see strong political leadership being necessary in order to develop policies on a whole-of-government basis and in order to create a shared vision of the type of society we wish to have in the future and to decide on the contribution of the public service to delivering on that vision.

The role of cabinet and the way it structures its business is centrally important in the effective management of cross-cutting issues. Apart from decluttering the agenda – in relation to which the Secretary General of the Department of the Taoiseach would have a role – there is a need for clear lines of responsibility from cabinet to ministers, ministers of state and to officials.

In relation to the Oireachtas, it will have an important role to play in the evaluation of cross-cutting initiatives with, possibly, the assistance of independent external experts. The relationship between committees of the Oireachtas and civil servants is in need of further clarification and would benefit from being more strategic and less adversarial. For their part, civil servants appearing before these committees should be encouraged to behave in a risk aware, and not a risk averse, manner. The nature of this relationship will become even more crucial in managing the cross-cutting agenda effectively.

There is a need for regular meetings of secretaries general and officials specifically in relation to the challenges of managing key cross-cutting issues effectively and in order to develop the 'corporate board' policy role of secretaries general. And, while secretaries general already meet with ministers through various cabinet sub-committees, there is a need to develop further these opportunities for political-administrative interface dialogue – particularly in relation to the cross-cutting agenda. Further development of this process would help to increase the level of trust and respect between both systems in their mutually complementary roles.

A renewed role for the SMI Implementation Group should be developed in which it would be chaired by the Department of the Taoiseach with a secretariat drawn from a range of departments and offices. Among other things, that group would have a role in ensuring that cross-cutting issues are on the political agenda and, equally, are prioritised on the civil service agenda. The group should also evaluate departmental strategy statements and the progress of SRAs over time.

New competencies, too, are necessary for the successful management of cross-cutting issues. Senior civil servants need to think in terms of a unified civil service – something which will be facilitated by the recent government decision to establish a Senior Executive Service. Equally, senior civil servants need to show leadership and to develop new competencies to manage new blocks of work from a cross-cutting perspective.

Above all, there is a crucial need to develop the role of the centre – i.e. the Department of Finance and the Department of the Taoiseach. First, they both need to bring clarity to their respective roles and develop new methodologies for co-operative working between them. Second, they need to take on a strong role in setting the agenda; the Department of Finance in terms of using the budgetary process to drive the cross-cutting agenda; the Department of the Taoiseach in terms of ensuring synergy between the political and administrative systems in prioritising the agenda.

Implementation strategies

We have also placed particular importance on strategies to ensure successful implementation of policies with a cross-cutting dimension and these have been outlined in detail in Chapter 4. Earlier in this report we highlighted the challenge of implementation which was identified by the PA Consulting Group in its review of SMI. The PA report made the point that

> The challenge for the modernisation programme in future will not be to consider 'what do we need to

change'. The work already done under SMI/DBG has explored these questions and provides an appropriate agenda moving forward. The real challenge will be to implement insights already secured. (PA, 2002, p.7).

Delivering Better Government highlighted concerns about the management of cross-departmental issues both in relation to the provision of policy advice and in the delivery of services. To achieve better co-ordination, DBG recommended the development and implementation of strategic result areas (SRAs) and the delivery of an integrated quality service. SRAs, which were defined as key areas of government activity spanning more than one department, are dependent on effective cross-cutting mechanisms both in their conception and in their delivery. As we make clear, this is also an area where progress to date has been less than satisfactory. For this reason we give special emphasis to SRAs as a key element of the effective implementation of the management of cross-cutting issues.

It is our hope that by grouping our recommendations around stakeholders' roles and implementation strategies, the challenge of implementation will be given the clearest possible focus. We also suggest that implementation of our recommendations, along with the unfinished parts of SMI/ DBG, as identified by PA Consulting Group in its report, should form part of the next phase of the modernisation programme.

Detailed recommendations

Our recommendations will entail some basic changes in how work is organised together with some changes to the culture and ethos of the civil service. For this reason, we stress that the recommendations must be considered as a whole – they are, in effect, a complete package of measures aimed at improving cross-cutting working.

Introduce a system of strategic result areas (SRAs) for government ...

The cabinet, with the advice and assistance of the Group of Secretaries General, should identify on a multi-annual basis a small number of its priorities in terms of strategic/whole-of-government/cross-cutting issues. These priorities need to be framed in clear and comprehensible terms. Objectives established at the level of the cabinet should cascade down to the level of individual departments/divisions and, in the process, link whole-of-government priorities with the individual departments' statements of strategy, divisional business plans and individual staff members' role profiles under the performance management development system.

... in which the management role of the centre of government is absolutely critical

The centre of government – the Departments of the Taoiseach and Finance – will have a crucial role to play in identifying and prioritising a small number of cross-cutting issues. In order to undertake this role effectively, there needs to be good communications structures in place to transfer political objectives to those departments. By using the budgetary process these departments should be proactive in ensuring that the financial and personnel resources required for delivery on cross-cutting issues are provided through either the lead department or agency or collectively to the departments and agencies involved.

Management of SRAs should be led by a single minister and department or agency

It is vital that the mandate of departments, as articulated in their statements of strategy, reflect fully the SRAs agreed at cabinet level. Based on our international experience, if these SRAs are to be managed successfully, there is a need for individual ministers, designated by the Taoiseach, to take the lead responsibility in relation to each SRA and to be account-able to cabinet by reporting on progress on a regular basis.

Management of SRA implementation programmes should be led by an identified official at an appropriate level of seniority

We have identified a number of issues, which are important to the successful implementation of an SRA programme. One of the most important is that a single individual within the lead department or agency should have overall responsibility for delivery of agreed results and that that individual should be appointed as a dedicated SRA manager.

SRA implementation programmes should have continuity in terms of staffing resources, expertise and experience

One of the features of inter-departmental committees is regular staff turnover due to promotions, staff transfers, decentralisation etc. If SRA programmes are to work effectively, human resource aspects must be prioritised and there must be a reasonable expectation that staff assigned to such programmes, and the accumulated expertise and experience which is built up over time, will not be taken away to meet departmental as opposed to SRA needs.

SRA delivery programmes should be supported by budgetary envelopes, where practical

The lead department or agency for each SRA will have an important role to play in relation to funding arrangements in order to ensure effectiveness in the delivery of objectives in this new regime which, by definition, will span the interests of more than one department. New financial procedures will be necessary to determine where the locus of control should lie in relation to the disbursement of individual SRA funds, and to deal with the need for new expenditure control arrangements in this multi-departmental environment and the costs of co-ordination associated with these new arrangements. Whatever arrangements are decided upon it is crucial that the level of budgetary autonomy available to the SRA management process should be clearly defined in advance.

There is a key role for a Senior Executive Service

We note the government decision for the creation of a Senior Executive Service (SES) and the preparatory work which is now underway in the Department of Finance. We cannot overemphasise the importance of an SES to the cross-cutting agenda. An SES will be critical in creating an environment in which individual departmental agendas are modulated by the demands of the whole-of-government agenda and in helping to remove some of the barriers to effective cross-cutting working.

An increased level of cross-departmental promotion to assistant secretary (director general) level and mobility between departments, at all levels, should be encouraged.

At present, although the Top Level Appointments Committee interviews across government departments and certain agencies for secretary general and assistant secretary level posts, only a minority of appointments to these posts are made from outside the home department (the department in which the vacancy arises). Seventy five percent of secretary general posts, 86 per cent of assistant secretary posts and 83 per cent of principal officer posts are filled from within home departments (Source: Department of Finance).

Greater mobility helps to break down silo-based attitudes and encourages informal networks – the latter being a strong feature in many of the countries studied.

Top management commitment to cross-departmental working needs to be developed and clearly communicated to line staff. Staff need to be aware that such working is valued. Management needs to build it into the departmental business planning process and the performance management development system which, in turn, will facilitate the development of the relevant cross-departmental working skills and competencies. All of this will be assisted by a career structure which clearly incentivises this kind of behaviour.

The operation of SRAs should be subject to separate external and internal evaluation

Progress in achieving results in relation to SRAs should be subject to parliamentary scrutiny and systematic evaluation. If possible, a joint Oireachtas committee tasked with this evaluation should be supported in its work through an expanded role for the Office of the Comptroller and Auditor General. Alternatively, an expert task force staffed by former senior civil servants/outside experts, with secretariat service provided by the Department of the Taoiseach, could undertake this task. In order to underpin the evaluation process, an amendment to the Public Service Management Act should be considered to put these arrangements on a legislative footing.

As a separate exercise, internal evaluation should also be undertaken, for example by seeking feedback from staff about the management of SRA projects to which they have contributed.

Implement a policy of regular review of agentisation process with a clear bias toward consolidation of structures under agreed policy frameworks

The Departments of Finance and the Taoiseach should review proposals for further fragmentation of government structures on a systematic basis. The benefits of establishing a new agency in any particular case should be carefully evaluated against the threats posed to effective cross-departmental working. Sponsoring departments should be required to review these conflicting demands before making proposals for development of further agencies. Where new agencies are developed, these should, where necessary, be subject to a central control framework which takes account of cross-cutting elements

Review departmental programmes multi-annually with a view to achieving exits

The Departments of Finance and the Taoiseach should systematically engage in a strategic process, ideally as part of an annual expenditure review, where departments seek to de-clutter agendas and structures by exiting from outmoded departmental programmes. The primary motivation here is not financial – it is to create space for new priorities and the better management of cross-cutting issues. The evaluation methodology will be critical to the effectiveness of these reviews.

Identify cross-cutting issues within departmental remits and assign responsibility for effective management of those issues going forward

There is a need for an annual process of identification of issues at departmental level which, potentially, might in time develop into SRAs. This process should act as a complement to the work at central government level. There is a need for central management of this process, which could be achieved by the Departments of the Taoiseach and Finance and operated through the Group of Secretaries General. The process itself, in turn, would help to develop the 'corporate board' policy role of secretaries general.

Bibliography

Accenture, *E-Government Leadership – Realising the Vision*, New York, 2002

Alcock, R.and Lenihan D.,*Opening the E-Government File: Governing in the 21st Century*, Ottawa: Centre for Collaborative Studies, 2001

Australians Working Together Programme (http://www. together.gov.au/aboutThePackage/default.asp.)

Aylward, S., Feely, S., Flanagan, J., Hennessy, M., Kearney, G., Molloy, R., O'Flynn, A., 'Implementing and Sustaining the Change Process in the Irish Public Sector', Dublin: *Administration*, vol. 49, no. 9 (Winter 2001-02), Institute of Public Administration.

Benton, S., Gaynor, M.C., Hynes, J., Mullen, F., *The Management of Cross-Cutting Issues in the Context of Public Sector Reform,* University of Dublin, Trinity College, School of Business Studies, 1996

Better Local Government, Dublin: Department of the Environment, 1996

Blair, Tony: Speech Launching Report on Electronic Government Services for the Twenty-First Century: Cabinet Office, London, September, 2002.

Boyle, R., *Evaluating Public Expenditure Programmes: Determining a Role for Programme Reviews*, Dublin: Institute of Public Administration, 1999

Boyle, R., *The Management of Cross Cutting Issues*, CPMR Discussion Paper 8, Dublin: Institute of Public Administration, 1999

Boyle, R., Fleming, S., *The Role of Strategy Statements*, CPMR Research Report 2, Dublin: Institute of Public Administration, 2000

Boyle, R., Humphreys, P.C., *A new Change Agenda for the Irish Public Service,* CPMR Discussion Paper 17, Dublin: Institute of Public Administration, 2001

Boyle, R., O'Riordan, J. and O'Donnell, O., *Longer Term Policy Development*, CPMR Paper 22, Dublin: Institute of Public Administration, 2002

Butler, M., *Evaluation in the Irish Health Sector*, Dublin: Institute of Public Administration, 2002

Byrne, D., J. Dully, D. Garvey, W. Kirwan, T. Mulherin, G. O'Hanlon, S. Rogers, O. Ryan, C. Treacy, B. Tuohy, M. Tutty , *Strategic Management in the Irish Civil Service: A Review Drawing on Experience in New Zealand and Australia*, University of Dublin, Trinity College, School of Business Studies, 1994

Cabinet Handbook (1998) Department of the Taoiseach, Dublin.

Chubb,B., *The Government and Politics of Ireland* 2nd ed., London: Longman, 1982

Collins, N. and Cradden, T., *Irish Politics Today*, Manchester: Manchester University Press, 1989

Communication from the Commission to the Council and European Parliament on a Community Immigration Policy, Brussels, 22/11/2000, Com(2000)757 – Final.

Crossing Boundaries: First Ottawa Working Session Summary, March 18, 2002, www.crossingboundaries/ca

Delivering Better Government, Second Report to Government of the Co-ordinating Group of Secretaries, Dublin: Stationery Office, 1996

Devlin, Liam St J., "The Devlin Report – An Overview", *Administration*, Vol. 17, No 4, Winter 1969, p.344, p.347

Department of the Environment and Local Government, Vision for Local Government, Dublin, 2000

Doz, Y., and Prahalad, C.K., 'A Process Model of Strategic Redirection in Large Complex Firms: The Case of Multinational Corporations'. in A. Pettigrew (ed) *The Management of Strategic Change,* Oxford: Blackwell, 1987

ESRI, *Medium Term Review 2001-2007*, ESRI, Dublin, 2001

Fanning, R., *The Irish Department of Finance 1922–1958*, Dublin: Institute of Public Administration, 1978

Finlay, F., *Snakes and Ladders*, Dublin: New Island Books, 1998

First Report to Government from the Co-ordinating Group of Secretaries, Dublin: Department of the Taoiseach, November 1994

Herd, R., *Coping with the Consequences of Ageing*, Paris: OECD Publications, 1999

Hill, C.W.L., and Jones, G.R., *Strategic Management Theory: an integrated approach*, 5th edition, Boston and New York: Hough Mifflin Company, 2001

Honahan, P., 'European and International Constraints on Irish Fiscal Policy', Paper presented to an ESRI Foundation for Fiscal Studies Conference, October 9, 2001.

ICTU: Factsheet, The Hague (2002) and www.ictu.nl

Kanter, R. M., *The Change Masters: Corporate Entrepreneurs at Work*, New York: International Thompson Business Press, 1983

Keoghan, J.F., McKevitt, D., 'Another set of Strategy Statements: what is the evidence of implementation?', *Administration*, Vol. 47, 1, pp.3-25, 1999

Laffan, B., *Organising for a Changing Europe: Irish Central Government and the European Union*, Dublin: The Policy Institute, Trinity College Dublin, 2001.

Lawrence, P.R., and Dyer, D, *Renewing American Industry* (1983), London: The Free Press, Collier McMillan

Lenihan, D. G., *Realigning Governance: From E-Government to E-Democracy*, Ottawa: Centre for Collaborative Studies, 2002

Lenihan, D. and D. Hume, *International Consultation Summary Report: The United States and Europe*, Ottawa: Centre for Collaborative Studies, 2002

Lillington, K., 'E-Government has Multiple Hurdles to Leap', *Irish Times*, 15 February 2002

Local Government in Denmark: (c) Kommunernes Landsforening 1999.

Markus, M. L. and R. Benjamin., 'The Magic Bullet Theory in IT – Enabled Transformation?', *Sloan Management Review*, Winter 1997

McDonagh, J., 'Electronic Service Delivery: The Challenge of Integrated Service, Dublin', Presentation to SMI Sub-Group on E-Government, 2001

Michalski, W., *The Future: What Policymakers have to think about*, Paris: OECD Publications, 1999.

Mintzberg, H., Quinn, J.B. and Gopshal, S., *The Strategy Process*, New York: Prentice Hall, Revised European Edition, 1998

Murray, J. A.,'Reflections on the SMI' (Working Paper) University of Dublin, Trinity College, School of Business Studies, November 2001

NESC, *Opportunities, Challenges and Capacities for Choice*: National Economic and Social Council, Dublin, 1999

New Connections – A strategy to realise the potential of the Information Society, Government Action Plan 2002, Dublin: Department of the Taoiseach

OECD , *Governance in Transition: Public Management Reforms in OECD Centres*, Paris, OECD, 1995

OECD (PUMA), *Globalisation – What Implications for Democratic Decision-making?*, OECD Publications, Paris, 1999

OECD, *Government of the Future*, OECD Publications, Paris, 2000

OECD, Programme for International Student Assessment (PISA), OECD Publications, Paris, 2000

OECD: Project on the Impact of E-government, PUMA, (2001) 10REV2, and http://www.oecd.org/EN/about/0,, EN-about-nodirectorate-no-no-no-13.FF.htlm

OECD (PUMA), *Public Sector Modernisation: A Ten Year Perspective* 13, OECD Publications, Paris, 2001

O'Connor, T., 'E-Government in Ireland: A Half-term Report Card – A Good Start but Many Risks Ahead', Version Talk, Vol. 2.1

Office Of The E-Envoy (UK), Channels Framework, October 2002.

Osborne, D. and Gaebler, T, *Reinventing Government: How the Entrepreneurial Spirit is Transforming the Public Sector,* Massachusetts: Addison-Wesley, 1992

PA Consulting Group, *Evaluation of the Progress of the Strategic Management Initiative / Delivering Better Government, Modernisation Programme*, PA Consulting Group, March 2002.

Perri 6: Holistic Government: London: Demos, 1997

Perri 6, Leat, D., Seltzker, K. and Stoker, G., *Governing in the Round: Strategies for Holistic Government*, London: Demos, 1999

Pettigrew, A.M., *The Awakening Giant*, Oxford: Blackwell, 1985

Pinder, A., *Channels Framework* (page 6), Office of the E-Envoy, London, October 2002

Pollitt, C. and Bouckaert, G., *Public Management Reform: A Comparative Analysis*, Oxford: Oxford University Press, 2000

Porter, M., 'Strategy and the Internet', *Harvard Business Review*, March 2001

Presidency Conclusions of Tampere European Council, 15/16 October, 1999

Presidency Conclusions of EU Council Meeting in Laeken, SN300-01, 14/15 December, 2001

Programme for National Recovery, Government Publications Office, Dublin, 1987

Programme for Prosperity and Fairness, Government Publications Office, Dublin,2000

Programme for Government, Government Publications Office, Dublin, 2002

Public Advisory Service Council, 11th Report, Government Publications Office Dublin, 1985

Public Services Management Act, 1997 (No. 27/1997), Dublin, Government Publications Office, 1997

Public Service Organisation Review Group Report, (Devlin Report). Government Publications Office, Dublin, 1969

Report of the Task Force on Integration of Local Government and Local Development Systems, Dublin: Department of the Environment and Local Government, 1998

'Report of the Implementation Group for the Information Society Action Plan', Unpublished report, CMOD, Department of Finance, Dublin 1999

Report of the Information Society Advisory Board to the Finnish Government on June 2001 published by the Ministry of Finance. – http:// www.infosoc.fi.

Review of the Centre, Report of the Advisory Group, Wellington: State Services Commission 2001 (http:/www.ssc.govt.nz/roc)

Rhodes, R.A.W, *Beyond Westminster and Whitehall,* London: Unwin, 1998

Rockart, J. F., Earl, M.J. and Ross, J.W., 'Eight Imperatives for the New IT Organisation', *Sloan Management Review*, Fall 1996

Rose, A. and Lawton, A. *Bureaucracy and Markets*, Essex: Pearson Education Ltd, 1999

Rose, A. and Lawton, A., *Public Sector Management*, New York: Prentice Hall, 1999

Sabel, C.F. and O'Donnell R., Paper presented to the OECD Conference on Devolution and Globalisation Paris: OECD Publications, 2000.

Scott, G., *Public Sector Management in New Zealand – Lessons and Challenges,* Canberra: Australian National University, 2001

Schick, A., 'Reflections on the New Zealand Model' (Paper based on a lecture at the New Zealand Treasury by Professor Allen Schick, August 2001 (http://www. treasury.govt.nz.academiclinkages/schick/paper.asp)

Schick, Allen, *Opportunity, strategy and tactics in reforming public management in Government of the future*, OECD, Paris,2000

Serving the Country Better: A White Paper on the Public Service, Government Publications, September 1985

Simpkins, K., *Budgeting and Accounting Issues: New Zealand*, Washington, International Federation of Accounts Public Sector Committee Executive Forum 1998 (p.11) (quoted in Report to Scottish Parliament Finance Committee, 20th meeting, 2001 (http:/ www.scottish. parliament.uk/official_report/cttee/finance-01/fip01-20.pdf)

Snow, C. C., Miles, R., Coleman, H. Jnr., 'Managing 21st Century Organisations', in *Organisational Dynamics*, Winter 1992

Stapleton, J., 'Civil Service Reform: 1969–1987', *Administration*, Vol 37, p.325, 1989

Stapleton J., 'Civil Service Reform', *Administration,* Vol. 38, 1991

Teahon, P., 'The implications for top management of managing strategic issues', paper delivered at National Conference of the Institute of Public Administration, Dublin, 1996

Thorninger, P., *The Danish E-Government Initiative: Digital Task Force,* Copenhagen, 2002

UK Cabinet Office, Speech by Prime Minister Tony Blair launching report on: Electronic Government Services for the Twenty-First Century: London, September 2000

UK Cabinet Office, Wiring It Up, a Performance and Innovation Unit Report, January 2000 (http://www. cabinet-office.gov.uk/innovation/2000/wiring/accounta-bility/04.htm

Visco, I., *Ageing Populations: Economic Issues and Policy Challenges,* OECD Publications, Paris, 2001.

Vitorino,A. European Commissioner for Justice and Home Affairs – Towards a common migration policy for the European Union Conference – 'Migration Scenarios for the 21st Century' Rome 12/7/00.

Wilson, Richard, 'Portrait of a Profession Revisited' (Speech delivered on 26 March 2002) London: Cabinet Office.

World Economic Forum, The Global Competitiveness Report, 2001-2002, Davos, 2001.

Index